The Causes and Consequences of Interest Theory

Cem Eyerci

The Causes and Consequences of Interest Theory

Analyzing Interest through Conventional and Islamic Economics

palgrave
macmillan

Cem Eyerci
Central Bank of the Republic
of Turkey
Ankara, Turkey

ISBN 978-3-030-78701-1   ISBN 978-3-030-78702-8 (eBook)
https://doi.org/10.1007/978-3-030-78702-8

This Palgrave Macmillan imprint is published by the registered company Springer Nature Switzerland AG
The registered company address is: Gewerbestrasse 11, 6330 Cham, Switzerland

Preface

Interest has always been a part of humans' daily economic life. Therefore, the concept of interest has attracted intense attention and been studied and discussed by philosophers, religious scholars, lawmakers, administrators, and economists, regarding almost all its economic, social, moral, and religious aspects. Receiving interest was mostly considered dishonorable, disrespectable, uncharitable, unjust, and the source of many evils. It was condemned in many societies for being a sin. For this reason, interest-based lending has always been restricted by the authorities through legislative, administrative, and financial arrangements, religion, and ethics. In cases when it was allowed, the rules of practicing interest were regulated heavily. However, despite all these concerns and regulations, interest has always been practiced in economic life.

By the seventeenth century, when the role of interest in economic life became more significant, scholars began to deal with the concept of interest more systematically, and many theories were developed on the nature of interest. Among many others, Böhm-Bawerk's comprehensive time-preference theory of interest presented causes for the existence of interest that may be claimed to be inherent.

On the other hand, a controversy emerged on the consequences of interest rate control in the relevant literature. It was claimed that prohibiting interest or limiting its rate, as a type of price control, has undesired distortive effects on the market in general. If so, the means-ends consistency in regulations may have to be reevaluated.

In this book, which is based on my Ph.D. dissertation, the concept of interest is studied in aspects of its meaning, history, and relevant theories. The time preference theory and the policy of interest rate control as a type of price control are introduced. The motivation for banning interest or limiting its rate and the instruments used in interest rate control are reviewed. Considering that the supporters of an interest-free economic system have the most explicit attitude against interest, the basics of the Islamic economic system are presented, and the prohibition of interest is analyzed. The approach and response of Islamic economists to the concept of the time value of money, to the causes of time preference asserted as the justifiers of interest, and to the claims on the distortive consequences of interest rate control are scrutinized.

I like to express my gratitude to Dr. Fuat Oğuz for his invaluable guidance and timely interventions that kept me on track and prevented the waste of effort on secondary issues, which is highly probable in such a work. I appreciate Dr. Ömer Demir for his considerable instructions, critiques, and, specifically, for his persistent encouragement to work continuously, which was one of the main motivations to run to the schedule. I owe thanks to Dr. Abdülkadir Develi for his comments that I benefited much from and Dr. A. Ömer Toprak for frequently reminding me of the task, which prevented me from slacking off. I also like to thank Ruth Jenner, Abarna Antonyraj, and their colleagues at Palgrave Macmillan for their kind assistance while finalizing the book and the referees, who reviewed the proposal and final version of the book. Finally, I am grateful to my family for easing many things through their support, understanding, and patience during this intensive period.

Ankara, Turkey Cem Eyerci

Contents

List of Figures

List of Tables

CHAPTER 1

Some Introductory Remarks

Lending has been a practice of humans' daily life presumably since the prehistoric ages well before the beginning of the usage of coin money. The first farmers, who lacked seed at sowing time but could not find a benefactor to receive the seed as gift or aid from, might have borrowed the seed. The lenders were lending to friends, neighbors, relatives, or needy people consentingly to receive back an amount of seed equal to the loan. On the other hand, some of these loans were made to receive back more at harvest-time (Homer 1963). The increment in the quantity of the loaned seed was called *interest* and had been paid for the other loaned goods and money as well, afterward.

Even though not complicated as it is in modern times, surprisingly still, the interest-based transactions were not merely comprised of ordinary and uniform practices. From the beginning, at least since the third millennium BC, there were standard values (Homer 1963) used in exchange, and beside the *basic interest*, *compound interest* was being practiced (Graeber 2011). The interest rates were changing in time and differentiating according to the place, loaned good, lender, borrower, and the purpose of the loan.

C. Eyerci, *The Causes and Consequences of Interest Theory*,
https://doi.org/10.1007/978-3-030-78702-8_1

1.1 The Legitimacy Problem

Along with the practice of interest-based transactions, a debate had continued on the legitimacy of interest. Since ancient times, many societies have condemned interest, and the authorities regulated interest-based transactions due to various concerns (Durkin 1993; Rougeau 1996; Visser and McIntosh 1998; Sharawy 2000; DeLorenzo 2006; Farooq 2012; Erdem 2018). It has been claimed that interest is an income received without working, is benefiting from the poor people, causes economic instability, enhances the inequality in the distribution of wealth, undermines the spirituality of people, and decreases the tendency to entrepreneurship, etc.

From ancient societies to the countries of the modern world, the authorities regulated interest-based transactions in aspects of execution, registration, and enforcement. However, the interventions were mostly to limit the rate of interest or to prohibit its practice. The interest rates were controlled by establishing upper limits changing in time and varying by the type of loan, lender, and borrower. In some periods of ancient Greece and ancient Rome, all kinds of interest-based lending were prohibited (Homer 1963; Visser and McIntosh 1998; Graeber 2011; Olechnowicz 2011).

In the regulation of interest-based transactions, besides legal and financial means, religious and ethical instruments were used in the past and being used today as well. Receiving interest is considered a sin and regulated almost in all religions (Visser and McIntosh 1998). In many societies, lending at interest has widely been considered unnatural, ethically disrespectable, and dishonorable (Homer 1963; Olechnowicz 2011; Graeber 2011). There have been laws regulating the interest-based transactions since ancient Babylonia's Code of Hammurabi (Homer 1963; Visser and McIntosh 1998; Graeber 2011; Geisst 2013). Today, in some countries, interest-bearing loans are entirely prohibited by law. In some other countries, including developed ones, some interest rate ceilings are defined (Glaeser and Scheinkman 1994; Reifner, Clerc-Renaud, and Knobloch 2010). The interest rates are also being controlled by the use of financial instruments such as lending to needy people at low-interest rates or free of interest (Homer 1963), and regulating the cost of the creditors through the reserve requirement ratios imposed by the central banks (Reifner et al. 2010).

1.2 The Causes of Interest

On the other hand, since ancient times, along with the evolving existence of interest and interventions of the authorities, the nature of interest has been studied much by philosophers, religious scholars, and lawmakers regarding its economic, moral, and religious aspects. In the seventeenth century, the role of interest in economic life became more significant by the increment in the mobility of money and the need for finance due to the developing trade. In consequence, the supporters of interest-based transactions, including mercantilists, physiocrats, and classical economists, came into the scene. In the new era, the scholars dealt with the concept of interest more, but particularly with its economic aspects rather than moral and religious aspects this time (Küçükkalay 2018). It was plausible why a needy borrower, who had no other option, was consentingly paying interest. However, the cause for the lenders' consideration of having the right to receive interest was not clear enough.

Thus, many theories were developed, attempting to explain the cause of the existence of interest. They mainly tried to answer the question: Why is there interest? The remaining part of the problem was in the social and political domain of the issue, and about interest's effect, necessity, justice, fairness, usefulness, and goodness (Böhm-Bawerk 1890). The scholars studied the concept of interest within the scope of the distribution theory. They defined interest as the income received from the capital, one of the four production factors.

There were monetary theories of interest, which dealt with the determination of interest rate by considering the quantity and velocity of money, and nonmonetary ones as well. From another aspect, the interest theories grounded on various causes, such as the productivity of capital, abstinence from the unproductive use of capital, human impatience, return from capital that is a form of stored labor, and exploitation of needy people.

The theories developed on the concept of *time preference* were among the most cited interest theories. Since Böhm-Bawerk is considered the founder of the modern theory of interest (Conard 1959; Potuzak 2016), his approach of time preference has particular importance. After severely criticizing several previous interest theories (Böhm-Bawerk 1890, 1903), Böhm-Bawerk (1930) developed a new one stating time preference as the focal point of the issue. The essential difference of his approach from the others' methodologies was the distinction he made between the positive and normative aspects of the concept of interest. The positive and normative distinction is very crucial in modern economics in which the first one focuses on *what is*, and the second one *what ought to be*. Böhm-Bawerk (1890) claimed that the cause of mistakes made in economists' works on the theory of interest was the lack of the abovementioned distinction.

Time preference in economics is defined as people's value attribution to present goods higher than future ones that have exactly the same quality and quantity. Thus, *interest* is the difference between the present and future values of a good.

Böhm-Bawerk (1930) specified three causes that can be considered valid in general, for the valuation of present goods higher than future ones. The first two causes were the preference for more consumption at present. People might prefer to consume more for consumption smoothing or because of the underestimation of the future due to the psychological traits of ordinary human beings. The third cause was not about the preference of present consumption but the desire for production more in value in the future.

Böhm-Bawerk's theory of interest has been in the focus of many scholars, and a number of them criticized it in various aspects (Walker 1892; Clark 1894; Fetter 1902; Fisher 1907; Mises 2006; Keynes 2013). However, after more than a hundred years of its assertion, the theory is still being worked on (Olson and Bailey 1981; Becker and Mulligan 1997; Frederick et al. 2002; Hülsmann 2002; Murphy 2003; Van Suntum and Neugebauer 2014).

1.3 Is Control of Interest a Good Idea?

Besides the debates on the legitimacy of interest-based transactions and the cause of interest, there has been a third controversy about whether controlling interest, namely prohibiting it or limiting its rate, is serving the purpose or not. Although there are scholars defending regulation of interest (Smith 1776; Keynes 2013; Metwally 1990; Glaeser and Scheinkman 1994; Rougeau 1996; Coco and De Meza 2009; Lee 2017; Cheng 2018), most of the economists are opposed to any ceiling on the rate of interest today (Durkin 1993). The opponents of limitations claim that interest rate controls have undesired distortive effects on the market.

The stance of the regulation-opponents originates from their consideration of the concept of *price control*. Price control is defined as the restriction on the price of a good or service imposed by an authority. Price ceilings prevent high prices over a limit as done in rent control, and price floors do not allow to transact at low prices under a limit as minimum wages (Coyne and Coyne 2015a). Price controls in a specific market are imposed for various purposes such as tackling inflation, protecting the consumers from black-market and exploitation, achieving equity in the workplace, preventing profiteering by property owners (Lipsey 1977; Schuettinger and Butler 1979; Bashar 1997; Bourne 2015; Miller 2015; Siebert 2015; Tabakoğlu 2016; Karadaği 2018).

Although used widely before, and still being used today, there have been doubts about the usefulness of price controls and even concerns about their adverse effects. Some controls are claimed to produce results just opposite to the intention and to have undesired distortive consequences on the market (Schuettinger and Butler 1979). Shortages; increment in bribery and black-marketing; reduction in investment; worsening in quality of existing properties; reduction in the construction of new estates; increment in cost of labor; reduction in labor demand; and increase in unemployment of the less qualified workers are some of the claimed negativities of price controls (Lipsey 1977; Schuettinger and Butler 1979; Booth and Davies 2015; Coyne and Coyne 2015b; Miller 2015; Siebert 2015; Snowdon 2015; Wellings 2015).

Yet another problem caused by price control that is argued is about the signaling role of the price in the market (Schmidtz 2016). Since price is considered a fast and effective transmitter (Sowell 1980) of a composite signal that is formed by all the relevant information, any control prevents this simplest way of the availability of required information in decision-making and increases uncertainty. Furthermore, the masking effect of price control may prevent to determine the real reasons for economic troubles (Coyne and Coyne 2015b).

Being defined as the price of the use of a loan, *controlling the rate of interest* is, no doubt, a form of price control. Then, interest rate control may have effects on the market, similar to the impacts of other price controls. A ceiling on interest under the market rate reduces the supply of loans, increases the demand, and causes a shortage. In such a case, although they are ready to borrow at a higher rate, the more needy borrowers fall into trouble in finding a loan. Due to the distinction made by lenders for being riskier, some of the borrowers that lost the opportunity to borrow are guided to usurers, pawnshops, and loan sharks (Durkin 1993; Ellison and Forster 2008; Rigbi 2013). On the other hand, the less needy borrowers, who borrow at a relatively lower interest rate, may not use the loan efficiently.

Regarding the signaling role of price, interest rate control prevents the transmission of some information, and a lack of information discourages the new lenders from entering the loan market and distorts the free competition.

The interest rate control may also have some macroeconomic negativity. The loss of the attraction of capital ownership may decrease savings, and so, the investment may decline. In consequence, the adversely affected output, employment, and income may reduce the total wealth (Durkin 1993).

1.4 Overview of the Content

It has been discussed throughout history whether receiving interest was licit. The philosophers, jurists, lawmakers, and economists either legitimized interest or objected to it.

The supporters of interest defined it as a necessity, or at least as a right, by asserting causes for its existence, referring to its usefulness in economics, and claiming that interest rate controls have distortive consequences in the market. The opponents, on the other hand, raised many reasons for its *evilness*, condemned it, and restricted interest-based transactions, either limiting interest rates or wholly prohibiting it. However, despite all concerns about it, whether it was allowed or not, interest has been more or less always practiced (Kuran 1995). As if inevitable, interest-based transactions made either legally or using loopholes in regulations or illicitly.

The controversy on interest is partially originating from the normative aspects of the interest-opponents' approaches. However, the opposing economists are increasingly attempting to justify their assertions in the positive domain. In this context, two interest-relevant issues deserve special attention and clarification, one on the side of *cause* and the other on the *effect* side.

The first ambiguity is about the reason for the existence of interest. Among many other causes claimed, time preference seems to be the most assertive one. In particular, Böhm-Bawerk's comprehensive theory presents an existential problem by grounding on the ordinary human attitude that can be claimed to be inherent.

The second controversial point is about the consequences of interest rate control. If the prohibition of interest or limiting its rate has undesired distortive effects on the market as claimed, means-ends consistency in regulations may be required to reevaluate.

Because the supporters of interest-free economic systems have the most explicit attitude against interest, the further success of the systems and the interest-free financial instruments they proposed requires plausible interpretations of these two issues. The conclusion may be either refuting or entirely or partially acknowledging these two assertions: Time preference is the cause of interest, and interest rate control has distortive consequences. Whatever the conclusion is, their arguments would be more accurate, and insofar as it is plausible, the arguments would be more convincing for others. Therefore, to be financially and socially efficient, any evaluation, judgment, or regulation on interest has to consider the coercive demand for the usage of interest and the consequences of interest rate control.

This book presents the concept of interest in aspects of meaning, history, and nature by focusing on its causes and consequences. Time preference, an important reason that seems inevitable, and the non-negligible implications of interest rate control are highlighted.

Although there are some other interest-free economic models and movements, Islamic economics may be considered to lead the way by its numerous supporters, relatively extensive literature, growing market, and actively operating instruments. Among other reasons that separate Islamic economics from conventional systems, the prohibition of interest is the most significant one. Since it is the most cited interest-free economic system, the basics of Islamic economics are reviewed. Specifically, the prohibition of interest in Islam is focused, and Islamic economists' interpretations of time preference and consequences of interest rate control are evaluated qualitatively.

In Chapter 2, the lexical meaning of interest and the definition of interest in economics are presented, and the history of interest since ancient times is reviewed.

In Chapter 3, the theoretical development in the concept of interest and the prominent interest theories are summarized. Then, Böhm-Bawerk's time preference theory of interest is introduced in detail by presenting his reason for developing a theory distinct from the existing ones, and the critiques of various scholars and the works testing the validity of the theory in the contemporary economy are reviewed.

In Chapter 4, the reasons for the prohibition of interest or limiting its rate are summarized. The legal, religious, ethical, and financial instruments used in the regulation of interest are presented in the second section.

In Chapter 5, the concept of price control concerning its mechanism and consequences is reviewed, and Steven Cheung's price control model, which applies to any price control regulation, is introduced. According to Cheung, for a correct evaluation of the consequences of a price control regulation, the specification of constraints proper to the real market practice should be available. However, the complexity of control regulations does not allow estimating the correct constraints. Cheung's theory attempts to propose a methodology that helps to investigate the relevant constraints of any price control rather than explaining the implications of a specific control. Lastly, the consequences of interest rate controls in various markets are evaluated.

In Chapter 6, after summarizing its historical background and its distinctions from conventional systems, the basic principles of the Islamic economic system are presented. Prohibition of interest, the main distinctive feature of Islamic economics, is reviewed regarding its origins from *the Quran* (the holy book) and *Sunnah* (practices of the Prophet). The traditional view of Islam on interest is presented by referring to the approach of *fiqh* (Islamic jurisprudence) to interest. The opposing views to the mainstream approach are summarized, and the instruments alternative to interest-based transactions and other devious ways used to overcome the prohibition are introduced. A chronological bibliography of Islamic economics on the concept of interest is also attached to the chapter in Appendix 6.1.

In Chapter 7, the Islamic economists' interpretations of the concept of the time value of money, the causes of time preference asserted as the justifiers of interest, and the claims about the distortive consequences of interest rate control are evaluated in detail, beginning from the twentieth mid-century.

Finally, in Chapter 8, the content of the previous chapters is summarized, and the findings are concluded.

References

Bashar, Muhammad Lawal Ahmad. 1997. "Price Control in an Islamic Economy." *Journal of King Abdulaziz University: Islamic Economics* 9: 29–52.

Becker, Gary S., and Casey B. Mulligan. 1997. "The Endogenous Determination of Time Preference." *The Quarterly Journal of Economics* 112 (3): 729–58.

Böhm-Bawerk, Eugen. 1890. *Capital and Interest: A Critical History of Economical Theory*. London: Macmillan.

———. 1903. *Recent Literature on Interest (1884–1899): A Supplement to "Capital and Interest."* New York: Macmillan.

———. 1930. *The Positive Theory of Capital*. New York: G.E.Stechert.

Booth, Philip, and Stephen Davies. 2015. "Price Ceilings in Financial Markets." In *Flaws and Ceilings: Price Controls and the Damage They Cause*, edited by Christopher Coyne and Rachel Coyne, 135–57. London: Institute of Economic Affairs.

Bourne, Ryan. 2015. "The Flaws in Rent Ceilings." In *Flaws and Ceilings: Price Controls and the Damage They Cause*, edited by Christopher Coyne and Rachel Coyne, 72–95. London: Institute of Economic Affairs.

Cheng, Hao. 2018. "The Death and Revival of Usury in China: An Institutional Analysis." *Journal of Economic Issues* 52 (2): 527–33.

Clark, John B. 1894. "The Genesis of Capital." *Hand Book of the American Economic Association* 9 (1): 64–68.

Coco, Giuseppe, and David De Meza. 2009. "In Defense of Usury Laws." *Journal of Money, Credit and Banking* 41 (8): 1691–1703.

Conard, Joseph W. 1959. *An Introduction to the Theory of Interest*. Berkeley: University of California Press.

Coyne, Christopher, and Rachel Coyne. 2015a. "Introduction." In *Flaws and Ceilings: Price Controls and the Damage They Cause*, edited by Christopher Coyne and Rachel Coyne, 1–7. London: Institute of Economic Affairs.

———. 2015b. "The Economics of Price Controls." In *Flaws and Ceilings: Price Controls and the Damage They Cause*, edited by Christopher Coyne and Rachel Coyne, 8–28. London: Institute of Economic Affairs.

DeLorenzo, Yusuf Talal. 2006. "Introduction to Understanding Riba." In *Interest in Islamic Economics: Understanding Riba*, edited by Abdulkadir Thomas, 1–9. New York: Routledge.

Durkin, Thomas A. 1993. "An Economic Perspective on Interest Rate Limitations." *Georgia State University Law Review* 9 (4).

Ellison, Anna, and Robert Forster. 2008. "The Impact of Interest Rate Ceilings: The Evidence from International Experience and the Implications for Regulation and Consumer Protection in the Credit Market in Australia." Policis. http://www.policis.com/pdf/Old/Australia_The_impact_of_interest_rate_ceilings_20080326.pdf.

Erdem, Ekrem. 2018. "Kur'an'da Riba (Faiz) Ayetlerinin Kademeli Nüzulü ve Üslubu: İslam'ın Ticaret, Infak ve Finans Sistemi Üzerinden Bir Inceleme [The Gradual Revelation and Style of the Riba (Interest) Verses in Quran: An Enquiry Regarding the Trade, Aid and Finance System of Islam]." In *İslam Iktisadı Perspektifinden Faiz [Interest from the Perspective of Islamic Economics]*, edited by Taha Eğri and Zeynep Hafsa Orhan, 1–51. İstanbul: İktisat Yayınları.

Farooq, Muhammad. 2012. "Interest, Usury and Its Impact on the Economy." *Dialogue* 7 (3): 265–76.

Fetter, Frank Albert. 1902. "The 'Roundabout Process' in the Interest Theory." *The Quarterly Journal of Economics* 17 (1): 163–80.

Fisher, Irving. 1907. *The Rate of Interest*. New York: Macmillan.

Frederick, Shane, George Loewenstein, and Ted O'donoghue. 2002. "Time Discounting and Time Preference: A Critical Review." *Journal of Economic Literature* 40 (2): 351–401.

Geisst, Charles R. 2013. *Beggar Thy Neighbor: A History of Usury and Debt*. University of Pennsylvania Press.

Glaeser, Edward L., and Jose A. Scheinkman. 1994. "Neither a Borrower Nor a Lender Be: An Economic Analysis of Interest Restrictions and Usury Laws." 4954. National Bureau of Economic Research.

Graeber, David. 2011. *Debt: The First 5000 Years*. New York: Melville House.

Homer, Sidney. 1963. *A History of Interest Rates*. Hoboken, NJ: Rutgers University Press.

Hülsmann, Jörg Guido. 2002. "A Theory of Interest." *Quarterly Journal of Austrian Economics* 5 (4): 77–110.

Karadaği, Ali Muhyiddin. 2018. *İslam Iktisadına Giriş [An Introduction to Islamic Economics]*. İstanbul: İktisat Yayınları.

Keynes, John Maynard. 2013. *The Collected Writings of John Maynard Keynes-The General Theory of Employment, Interest and Money*, vol. 8. New York: Cambridge University Press.

Küçükkalay, Abdullah Mesud. 2018. *İktisadi Düşüncede Faiz [Interest in Economic Thought]*. Konya: Çizgi Kitabevi.

Kuran, Timur. 1995. "Islamic Economics and the Islamic Subeconomy." *Journal of Economic Perspectives* 9 (4): 155–73.

Lee, Joanne. 2017. "Should Interest Rates Be Regulated or Abolished? The Case for the Abolition of Usury." *The Western Australian Jurist* 8: 227–62.

Lipsey, Richard G. 1977. "Wage-Price Controls: How to Do a Lot of Harm by Trying to Do a Little Good." *Canadian Public Policy* 3 (1): 1–13.

Metwally, Mukhtar M. 1990. "Towards Abolishing the Rate of Interest in Contemporary Islamic Societies." *Journal of King Abdulaziz University: Islamic Economics* 2 (1): 3–23.

Miller, Robert C.B. 2015. "Price Ceilings: Ancient and Modern." In *Flaws and Ceilings: Price Controls and the Damage They Cause*, edited by Christopher Coyne and Rachel Coyne, 29–44. London: Institute of Economic Affairs.

Mises, Ludwig von. 2006. *Human Action: A Treatise on Economics*. Indianapolis: Liberty Fund.

Murphy, Robert P. 2003. "Unanticipated Intertemporal Change in Theories of Interest." New York: New York University, Graduate School of Arts and Science.

Olechnowicz, Cheryl A. 2011. "History of Usury: The Transition of Usury through Ancient Greece, the Rise of Christianity and Islam, and the Expansion of Long-Distance Trade and Capitalism." *Gettysburg Economic Review* 5: 97–109.

Olson, Mancur, and Martin J. Bailey. 1981. "Positive Time Preference." *Journal of Political Economy* 89 (1): 1–25.

Potuzak, Pavel. 2016. "What Can We Learn from the Böhm-Bawerkian Theory in the World of Zero Interest?" Available at SSRN 2865082. https://ssrn.com/abstract=2865082.

Reifner, Udo, Sebastien Clerc-Renaud, and RA Michael Knobloch. 2010. "Study on Interest Rate Restrictions in the EU." ETD/2009/IM/H3/87. Institut für Finanzdienstleistungen.

Rigbi, Oren. 2013. "The Effects of Usury Laws: Evidence from the Online Loan Market." *Review of Economics and Statistics* 95 (4): 1238–48.

Rougeau, Vincent D. 1996. "Rediscovering Usury: An Argument for Legal Controls on Credit Card Interest Rates." *University of Colorado Law Review* 67 (1): 1–46.

Schmidtz, David. 2016. "Are Price Controls Fair?" *Supreme Court Economic Review* 23 (1): 221–33.

Schuettinger, Robert L., and Eamonn F. Butler. 1979. *Forty Centuries of Wage and Price Controls: How Not to Fight Inflation*. Washington, DC: Heritage Foundation.

Sharawy, Hesham M. 2000. "Understanding the Islamic Prohibition of Interest: A Guide to Aid Economic Cooperation between the Islamic and Western Worlds." *Georgia Journal of International and Comparative Law* 29 (1): 153–79.

Siebert, W. Stanley. 2015. "The Simple Economics of Wage Floors." In *Flaws and Ceilings: Price Controls and the Damage They Cause*, edited by Christopher Coyne and Rachel Coyne, 45–71. London: Institute of Economic Affairs.

Smith, Adam. 1776. *The Wealth of Nations*. The Electric Book.

Snowdon, Christopher. 2015. "Minimum Unit Pricing." In *Flaws and Ceilings: Price Controls and the Damage They Cause*, edited by Christopher Coyne and Rachel Coyne, 177–97. London: Institute of Economic Affairs.

Sowell, Thomas. 1980. *Knowledge and Decisions*. New York: Basic Books.
Tabakoğlu, Ahmet. 2016. *İslam İktisadına Giriş [An Introduction to Islamic Economics]*. İstanbul: Dergah Yayınları.
Van Suntum, Ulrich, and Tom Neugebauer. 2014. "Böhm-Bawerk Meets Keynes: What Does Determine the Interest Rate, and Can It Become Negative?" *University of Münster, Center of Applied Economic Research Münster Discussion Paper* 65: 127–45.
Visser, Wayne A.M., and Alastair McIntosh. 1998. "A Short Review of the Historical Critique of Usury." *Accounting, Business & Financial History* 8 (2): 175–89.
Walker, Francis A. 1892. "Dr. Boehm-Bawerk's Theory of Interest." *Quarterly Journal of Economics* 6: 399–416.
Wellings, Richard. 2015. "Regulation of Rail Fares." In *Flaws and Ceilings: Price Controls and the Damage They Cause*, edited by Christopher Coyne and Rachel Coyne, 118–34. London: Institute of Economic Affairs.

CHAPTER 2

The Concept of Interest: Meaning and History

Interest had existed long before the beginning of the efforts to understand and define it. In the first section of this chapter, the literal meaning of the word *interest* is presented, and its ascribed meaning as an economic term is scrutinized in aspects of various definitions and types. The history of interest is reviewed beginning from the ancient times in terms of the rates, causes, and regulations of interest, and the enforcement tools of defaulted loans, in the second section.

2.1 What Is Interest?

The word *interest* means *to be between* as a combination of two words; *inter* means *between* and *esse* means *to be*. As Online Etymology Dictionary (2019) defines, the word *interest* was used in meanings of "legal claim or right; a concern; a benefit, advantage, a being concerned or affected ..." (entry of *interest*) in the middle of the fifteenth century. The word *interest* was derived from the Latin word of *interesse*, which initially meant a penalty of a defaulted or late repaid loan. However, the origin of *interest* was closely related to the meaning of *usury* that was defined as the repayment of a loan exceeding the principal in medieval Europe (Persky 2007). In time, *usury* evolved to mean *excessive interest* in most of the world by the adoption of the meaning of *interest* to be the increment in the repaid loan at an acceptable rate.

C. Eyerci, *The Causes and Consequences of Interest Theory*,
https://doi.org/10.1007/978-3-030-78702-8_2

Although the word has been used in some other meanings in the past and today as well (Table 2.1), the earliest relevant usage was in the sixteenth century ("Interest in Online Etymology Dictionary" 2019), the same as in its present meaning of *payment for the use of borrowed money*.

At present, the relevant meaning of *interest* is defined in Merriam-Webster (2019) dictionary as "a: charge for borrowed money generally a percentage of the amount borrowed, b: the profit in goods or money that is made on invested capital, c: an excess above what is due or expected" (entry of *interest*). The Oxford Advanced Learner's Dictionary (2000) preferred a single definition as "the extra money that you pay back when you borrow money or that you receive when you invest money" (p. 625). Even though the dictionaries define interest as the increment in money lent, it is clear that interest-bearing transactions of goods besides money were made in the past and are still being partially made today.

However, some scholars used the word *interest* in various meanings as an economic term (Table 2.2). Irving Fisher (1930) defined interest as the name of all types of income. Joseph Schumpeter's (1934) definition was narrower than Fisher's was, that named all returns, except the wages, as interest.

Table 2.1 The change in the meaning of *interest* over time

Era	*Meaning of* interest
The Latin origin	*Interesse*: A penalty of a defaulted or late repaid loan (*inter*: between + *esse*: to be)
Medieval	The repayment of a loan exceeding the principal
Fifteenth century	Legal claim or right; a concern; a benefit, advantage, a being concerned or affected *(Online Etymology Dictionary)*
Sixteenth century	Payment for the use of borrowed money *(Online Etymology Dictionary)*
Today	a. Charge for borrowed money generally a percentage of the amount borrowed b. The profit in goods or money that is made on invested capital c. An excess above what is due or expected *(Merriam-Webster Dictionary)* The extra money that you pay back when you borrow money or that you receive when you invest money *(The Oxford Advanced Learner's Dictionary)*

Table 2.2 Some definitions of interest made by various scholars

Scholar	*Definition of interest*
Turgot (1766)	The price of the use of loaned money
Smith (1776)	The revenue derived from the stock that lent to others
Senior (Medema and Samuels 2003)	The revenue of the lender for abstaining from present consumption
James Mill (Conard 1959)	The revenue of stored labor, a form of capital
Böhm-Bawerk (1890)	The income that flows from the capital
Fisher (1930)	The name of all types of income
Schumpeter (1934)	All returns, except the wages
Knight (Conard 1959)	Interest and rent are the same

Some other scholars regarded interest as it is commonly accepted: *the increment in a loan when it is paid back*, but made some additional definitions due to their approaches to the nature of interest. Frank H. Knight, for example, asserted that interest and rent are the same (Conard 1959). Anne Robert Jacques Turgot (1766) defined interest as the price of the use of loaned money. Adam Smith (1776) described interest as the revenue derived from the stock that lent to others. Nassau W. Senior defined interest as the lender receives for her abstaining from present consumption (Medema and Samuels 2003). As a final example, according to James Mill, interest is the revenue of stored labor, a form of capital (Conard 1959).

No matter how the word *interest* is defined, one should possess an asset to be able to lend. Capital, the mentioned asset to be lent, is characterized by Böhm-Bawerk (1890) as "… a complex of goods that originate in a previous process of production, and are destined, not for immediate consumption, but to serve as means of acquiring further goods" (p. 6). Since the current consumption vanishes before being used as capital and the land is not produced, Böhm-Bawerk excluded these two assets from the scope of capital. Thus, Böhm-Bawerk also made a distinct definition of interest: *the income that flows from capital is interest*.

On the other hand, there are various breakdowns of interest (Fig. 2.1). *Gross interest*, for example, is the increment in the loan paid back by the borrower, which also involves the transaction costs such as taxes and risk premiums. Differently, *net interest* is the real income of the lender that received for the lent capital, after the deduction of the costs from the gross

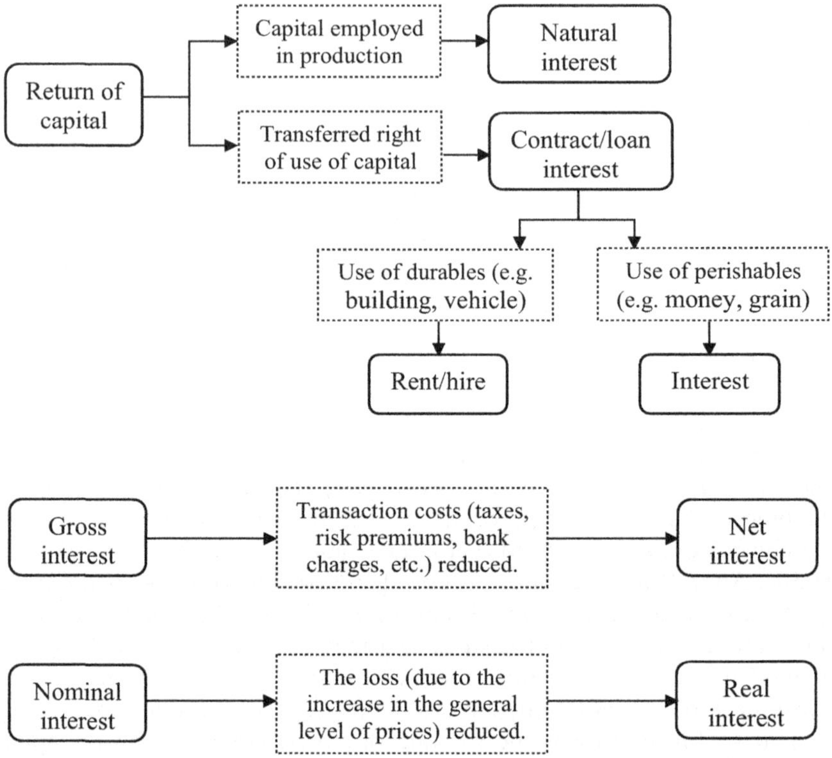

Fig. 2.1 Various breakdowns of interest

interest. In other words, when there is a transaction cost, the interest rates of a loan for a lender and a borrower are not equal.

Another breakdown is of *natural interest* and *contract* or *loan interest*. The value of a product increases by the use of capital in production. In general, the increment in the value of the product is higher than the value of capital used. The increment above the invested capital is the profit of capital, namely *natural interest*. The owner of capital does not always employ it himself in production but gives it to someone else against a fixed remuneration. The remuneration received from capital that is durable such as building, vehicle, or tool, is called hire or rent. When the capital is perishable as money, grain, or another commodity, the income is called interest. Both rent and interest are called *contract* or *loan interest* (Böhm-Bawerk 1890).

The distinction between *nominal interest* and *real interest* should also be considered. Nominal interest is simply the interest on a loan or investment. In case of the existence of inflation, the real value of the capital at the lending or investment time, especially when capital is money, cannot be kept at the end of the lending or investment period. The real interest is the normalized nominal interest by the inflation rate.

The interest rate, which is the ratio of the amount of increment to the amount of capital lent, has some determinants. These determinants are essential to understand what the rate means. The interest rate may change according to the

- time, maturity, size, place, and legality of the loan,
- taxability of the interest income,
- level of the reliability of the borrower,
- existence of indemnity,
- institutional identity of the lender.

Within the scope of this book, unless otherwise specified, that is intended by *interest* is *net* and *real interest*, but not the gross, natural, rent based loan or nominal interest.

2.2 The History of Interest

Lending has been utilized in economic life since the prehistoric ages. Although the usage of money as the coin had begun at the first millennium BC, lending had existed well before the emergence of money. The Neolithic farmers, who had given seed to others by expecting return, might be the first lenders. The amount of repayment for the loans to a friend, neighbor, or relative could be equal to the amount lent. However, some of these lenders received back more at harvest-time. Similarly, cattle had been lent and received with their calves at the repayment time (Homer 1963). The increased part of the seed and the calves of the cattle were called *interest*, and requested for loans of other goods and money as well, in many ancient, medieval, and modern societies.

Metals like gold, silver, lead, bronze, and copper had begun to be loaned at interest by the development of mining. The exchange of metals had been made by weight before the emergence of money (Homer 1963).

There are findings regarding the practice of interest in Mesopotamia, Ancient India, Ancient Greece, Ancient Rome, Byzantium, and Medieval Europe as it is briefed in the following. The Abrahamic religions (Judaism, Christianity, and Islam) strictly intervened in the practice of interest, and their approach to the issue has to be considered to comprehend how the perception of interest and its practice evolved to present conception.

The rate of interest changed in time and varied due to the type of the loan (personal, mortgage, maritime, commerce, etc.) and identity of the borrower (citizen, merchant, state, etc.) and lender (banker, church, pawnbroker, etc.).

2.2.1 Mesopotamia

In ancient Sumer, from the third millennium BC to 1900 BC, grain and silver were standard values (Homer 1963). The Sumerian writings, available today, were mostly about records of commercial transactions and contracts, including interest-based loans. In the twenty-fourth century BC, a Sumerian legal code regulated the loan transactions and freed the people imprisoned for the debt not paid back (Vincent 2014). The Sumerian people were familiar with loans not only at basic interest but also at compound interest (Graeber 2011). The usual rate of interest for a loan of barley was $33\frac{1}{3}$, and for a loan of silver was 20% (Homer 1963).

The Sumerian financial practices that survived until the Babylonian era took place in the Code of Hammurabi, which came into force circa 1800 BC. The Code allowed lending at interest, but a maximum interest rate was defined for each type of loan. It was mandatory to make the loan contracts before an officer and witnesses in Babylonia. If not, the lender could not claim anything. The lender also lost the repayment if an interest rate over the maximum level was defined. Pledges and sureties were used to protect the lender in a case of default. People such as wife, concubine, children, and slaves or possessions like land, house, and door were allowed to pledge. The slavery of such people was possible only for three years. The limit on the slavery period has extended later (Homer 1963).

The loans were usually in grain and silver. Similar to the Sumerian era, the maximum interest rate on loans of grain (one third per annum) was higher than on loans of silver (20% per annum) for more than a thousand years. Although the usual maximum interest rate on loans of silver was 20%, there were also examples as 25 and 12% per annum. The lenders were not only the individuals, but the temples were also lending. The temples used lower levels of interest rates such as 20% for loans of barley, and 6¼% for loans of silver to help the poor people. Even the temples lent without interest in some cases. The interest rates were higher in the neighboring countries of Babylonia in that era (Homer 1963).

In the period of 732–625 BC, when the Assyrians dominated, the legal maximum interest rate remained the same in Babylonia. However, the interest rates in Assyria itself were not the same as the Babylonian rates. Although there is no evidence of any interest rate limits used in Assyria in the ninth and eighth century BC, the normal interest rates on grain loans were 30–50%, and on silver loans were 20–40% per annum (Homer 1963).

Then, in the Neo-Babylonian Empire, from 625 to 539 BC, the allowed maximum interest rate on grain loans was reduced to 20%, and it became equal to the rate on silver loans. Lending with interest rates higher than the defined maximum level was rarely allowed. However, usually, the rates in the loan market were below the maximum rates of interest. There were examples that professional creditors lent at 11⅔% and some others lent at interest rates varying between 16⅔ and 20% (Homer 1963).

The loans at interest survived for thousands of years in Mesopotamia with the frequent interventions of the authorities. However, the interventions were not only for the regulation of lending. For the restoration of justice and equity, the protection of widows and orphans, or other similar reasons, the debts were abolished several times in Sumer, Babylonia, and Assyria (Graeber 2011).

2.2.2 Ancient India

The earliest information about the existence of loans at interest in ancient India is of the period of the twentieth to fourteenth century BC. It is known more about the loans at interest in the later centuries of seventh to first BC. A Hindu law was made, and lending at interest became forbidden for the upper classes such as priests and the warriors. On the contrary, the Hindu temples were allowed and commonly lent at interest. In the second century AD, the Laws of Manu, the Hindu code, defined the interest rates above the legal rate to be usurious and such attempts to be against the law. On the other hand, in medieval India, the Hindu law emphasized that the one who could not repay a loan would be reborn as a slave of her lender or her horse or ox. The same attitude was observed in Buddhism (Visser and McIntosh 1998; Graeber 2011).

The earlier rules limited the interest rate of loans at 15% per annum, except for commercial loans. Then, various limits were defined for each caste in the range of 24–60% per annum (Graeber 2011).

2.2.3 Ancient Greece

The population lived around the Aegean Sea from 2400 to 1200 BC is known to reach a high level of economic activity. However, there is not any information about lending made at interest. On the other hand, the Greek poet Hesiod mentioned the interest-free seed loans. In this period, cattle were the standard values at the beginning. Later, metals were begun to use for exchange. In the seventh century BC, the Greeks developed an economic system based on trade. The loans at interest were used much in commerce (Homer 1963).

At the beginning of the sixth century BC, the farmers faced massive economic troubles. They were producing but could not keep most of their production. Slavery for non-repaid loans was allowed and frequently observed. In 594 BC, Solon, a prominent wise man, was empowered by Athens with legislative power for a limited period to revise the laws. Solon made radical reforms. Many debts were canceled or reduced by the revision of laws. The slaves for unpaid loans were released. The limits and restrictions on the interest rates were removed. However, personal slavery established for not paid loans was forbidden. Instead, the loans began to be secured by real estate. Bankers that lent to individuals and states were prevalent in the fourth century BC. Various assets such as state revenues, cargoes, pawns, and real estate were used to secure the loans. Besides, unsecured loans were also made (Homer 1963).

In the fourth century BC, during the lifetime of Aristotle, it was believed that the loans aiming profit were unnatural and dishonorable. Aristotle classified wealth acquiring in two types. The necessary and honorable one was household management. The retail trade in which people gain from one another was regarded to be unnatural. Mostly the deal of money, lending at interest, had been hated. Money was for exchange only (Olechnowicz 2011). Even so, this belief did not resolve the existence of loans at interest.

In ancient Greece, interest rates highly varied in time. The rates differed among cities and were not the same for different types of loans. The normal interest rate of loans of silver in Athens in Solon's time (the sixth century BC) was 16–18%. It was 6–10% in the second century BC and 8–9% in the first century AD. The interest rate on the real estate loans varied between 6⅔ and 18% in the period of fifth to second century BC. The interest rate on loans to cities was 7–48%, to industry and commerce was 12–38%, and the rate on the earnings of endowment funds was 6–16%. There were some other types of lending, such as personal and usurious loans. The interest rates of these types varied in a wide range, for example, 36% in the fifth century BC, various rates from 10 to 9000% in the fourth, and 24% in the third century BC (Homer 1963).

2.2.4 Ancient Rome

The Romans of high status had income from landholding and usury, but the activities of commerce and industry were regarded dishonorable and left to the former slaves (Baumol 1990) and foreigners. That may be the reason for observing fewer records of interest rates in ancient Rome, compared to ancient Greece. The first known form of money in ancient Rome was cattle and some other animals. By the fifth century BC, copper and bronze became to be used for exchange. Rome began to use the silver coin in the second century BC (Homer 1963).

Before 443 BC, the loans were secured by slavery, and the defaulted debtors were sold in foreign lands. In 443 BC, Twelve Tables codified Roman law. According to the Tables, the debtors were allowed for thirty days to pay. In case of default, the lender was able to seize and fetter the debtor but had to feed him. On the other hand, creditors receiving an interest higher than the legal maximum of 8⅓% per annum had to pay a fine. In 347 BC, the maximum rate was reduced to 4⅙% per annum, and around 342 BC, it again increased to 8⅓% (Homer 1963). Once in 340 BC, the loans at interest were totally banned within the Lex Genucia reforms, but this did not prevent the existence of loans at interest, and the rules changed back again (Visser and McIntosh 1998).

In 326 BC, the imprisonment of Romans for debt became forbidden for the first time. In 192 BC, the foreigners were also covered by the law. Rome was the financial center of the world by the first century BC (Homer 1963).

The legal maximum interest rates of Rome were around 12% from the first century BC to the fourth century AD. Besides, the normal interest rates varied in a range of 4–12% in the same period. The interest rates in the Roman provinces were quite different from the ones in Rome (Homer 1963).

It is a general acceptance that the loans were not at interest in Egypt until the eighth century BC. Lending was probably among the neighbors only, and it was free of interest (Graeber 2011). During the Roman domination, in the fifth century BC, the interest rate on the loan of grain was 100%, and of silver was 85% in Egypt. In the second century BC, the rates were 5–10% in Egypt and 8–12% in Asia Minor. In the second century AD, the interest rates were 6–50% in Egypt, 6–12% in Asia Minor, and 5–12% in Roman Africa (Homer 1963).

2.2.5 *Byzantium*

About the era of the Eastern Roman Empire, regarding interest, only the legal limits are known. Since the interest rates were considered too high, the legal maximums of interest rates were reduced to a range of 4–8% by the Justinian Code in the sixth century. Bankers and ordinary citizens were allowed to charge 8 and 6%, respectively. The interest rates of maritime loans per voyage and the loans of commodities payable in kind were limited to 12%. The interest of the loans to churches and foundations were lower, 3%. Besides, accumulated interest was not allowed to exceed the principal. The legal limits in the seventh and eighth centuries were the same as in the sixth century. In the ninth and tenth centuries, the legal limits increased to $8^1/_3$–$11^1/_8$% range (Homer 1963).

2.2.6 *Interest in the Abrahamic Religions and Medieval Europe*

Considering that more than half of the world population is composed of the adherents of the Abrahamic religions (Judaism, Christianity, and Islam), their approaches to the concept of interest deserve a close examination. More importantly, the evolution of the perception of interest and its practice into the present conventional conception has taken place essentially in Christian Europe and continued in the Western World. On the other hand, presumably, the most prominent interest-free approach that is claimed to be an alternative to the conventional view has emerged within Islamic economics thought.

Christianity and Islam forbade lending at interest. However, Judaism defines some exceptions. The Jews were not allowed to lend at interest to other Jews and to non-Jews, who believed in the relevant rules of Torah, but it was permitted to make interest-based transactions with others (Visser and McIntosh 1998).

After the emergence of Christianity, an ambiguity arose about the legitimacy of interest due to various contradicting decrees in old and new testaments. The result of the attempts to overcome the uncertainty was against interest, and in the fourth century AD, the Roman Catholic Church prohibited to lend at interest for the clergy (Visser and McIntosh 1998).

Circa 800, during the reign of Charlemagne, the earlier prohibitions were adopted as state law, and the interest restriction was extended, covering all people (Küçükkalay 2018). However, Jews were not included in the prohibition and were accepted as legal moneylenders by the Church (Geisst 2013). After about 300 years, in the eleventh century, the scholars examined the practice of interest in detail, and it was declared that lending at interest was a form of robbery, so it was a sin. In the twelfth century, Pope Alexander III decreed that forward sales at a price above the cash price were usurious. According to the decree, usurers were guilty of being uncharitable and avarice, and sinners against justice. Therefore, they had been excommunicated (Homer 1963). The decree also widened the scope of the prohibition of interest. The lending types that were legal previously and similar to interest-bearing loans were prohibited (Küçükkalay 2018).

The essential attitude did not change much until the emergence of Protestantism in the sixteenth century. Within the thought of Reformation, Luther, Calvin, and others asserted that interest should not be condemned, and thus the prohibition of interest was removed gradually. However, some of the pioneers of the new approach had reservations on the legitimacy of interest. For example, although he came to be known as wholly supporting it, Calvin defined cases in which interest remained sinful. Disregarding any reservations, the sympathy to interest spread out, and by the changed attitude of the authorities on interest, usury was redefined as the interest above the acceptable rate (Visser and McIntosh 1998).

While the prohibition of interest was weakening in Protestant countries, the tightness of the Church policies continued until the eighteenth century in the Catholic world. Even though some credit forms such as insurance contracts and state loans were allowed and used along a few centuries, the Catholic Church came to approve new lending forms that were easing the usage of interest in the eighteenth century (Homer 1963; Chown 1996). In the nineteenth century, it was decreed that everyone was allowed to receive interest at a rate not more than the defined maximum (Homer 1963), and it is still the view of the Church (Visser and McIntosh 1998).

It should be noted that various prohibitions and regulations of interest made by the Church during many centuries did not merely stem from religious motivations. In some periods, some merchants, who were able to use instruments for evading the Church's regulations, supported the prohibitions. Thus, the others, lacking the abovementioned instruments, were kept away from the market. In consequence of the ban on interest, the implicit interest rate observed was higher than the rate that would be if it were legal; a small group of merchant bankers took the monopoly power; the pawnbrokers that publicly lent at interest emerged. The administrators, privileged merchants, and the Church shared the rents that originated from the prohibition of interest (Koyama 2010).

The *acceptable interest rate* that was not exceeding an upper limit has been a much-debated issue all the time, and defining it is still an unsolved problem. However, today, the Church's decree does not influence the practice of law much in most of the Christian populated countries.

Despite the abovementioned and many other regulations of religious and administrative authorities for the prohibition of interest, the interest-bearing practices always existed in Europe illegally or semi-legally. Along with the revival of trade and industry in the eleventh century, the need for the finance of economic activities increased, and some new forms of lending developed. The supporters of interest emerged by using some loopholes in the law and contradictions in the Church's arguments (Visser and McIntosh 1998).

The new instruments helped to meet the need for lending but not explicitly considered a sin. For example, the pawnbrokers, who were Jews in general and often tolerated and licensed through heavy fees, made secured consumption loans at an interest rate of 32½–300% per annum. State loans might be another example. Some states forced the wealthy citizens to lend to the state in proportion to their wealth. The states were defining the date of repayment, and annual payments were made to the lenders as gifts. The rate of interest was low, and nobody was voluntary for making such loans. In the fourteenth century, a practice was developed by the partnerships that one partner was insuring the investor partner against loss. In the sixteenth century, the Church unofficially approved the practice of profit insurance, and the interest received from such investments was used to support the needy people and the Church (Homer 1963).

The records of interest rates became available again, after a long time, in the twelfth century. In England, the Jews were the primary lenders. The usual interest rate was changing in a range of 43⅓–120% due to the quality of the security. The maturity of the loans was not longer than a year, and the often-used interest rates were weekly rates. At the end of the century, the interest rate was between 10 and 16% in the Netherlands, and 20% in Genoa (Homer 1963).

In the thirteenth and fourteenth centuries, the types of loans diversified. There were loans to princes, personal loans, commercial loans, deposits, mortgages, and loans to states. The interest rates varied due to the type of loan and state. For example, the interest rates were in a range of 5–40% in the thirteenth century. The upper limits defined for pawnshops in some states were higher up to 300%. The variation of the interest rates among the loan types and the countries remained similar during a few centuries. In the second half of the seventeenth century, the interest rates of various loan types decreased to some extent. In these years, the interest rates of short-term commercial loans were 1¾–4½% in the Dutch Republic and 3–6% in England. Short-term deposits had interest rates of 3–4% in the Dutch Republic and 4–6% in England. The interest rates used in mortgages and other long-term debts were 3–12½% in the Dutch Republic, 4–6% in England, and 5–8⅓% in France (Homer 1963).

The traditional Islamic view on interest did not become evident during the lifetime of the Prophet, in the early decades of the seventh century. *Riba,* which means increase, addition, or expansion (Chapra 1996), is prohibited both in the *Quran* (the holy book) and in *Sunnah* (practices of the Prophet). However, there has been a long-continued debate on the scope of riba after the Prophet. Although there are many others, the widely accepted definition for riba is "*any increment in the amount of borrowed money or asset on the repayment day.*" According to this traditional and most common view, riba means interest. Since interest is not allowed, at any rate, a riba-based or interest-based lending is the same as usury.

Although not honored much, there have been various approaches distinct from the traditional one. Some scholars differentiate the loans for consumption from the ones for production. They claim that the income from the former is not allowed due to being riba, and the income from the latter is allowed since it is an interest. Some others assert that the simple interest is not implied by riba, but the inhibited action is receiving compound interest. Another approach defines the prohibited riba to be the same as usury or excessive interest, but excludes interest at an acceptable rate from riba and legitimates it.

The interest rates of some transactions in Ancient times and Medieval Europe are summarized in Table 2.3.

Table 2.3 Some annual interest rates practiced in Ancient times and Medieval Europe

Era		*Normal rates (%)*	*Lower rates (%)*	*Excessive rates (%)*
Mesopotamia-Sumer	3rd millennium BC to 1900 BC	$33\frac{1}{3}$ (for grain) 20 (for silver)		
Mesopotamia-Babylonia	More than 1000 years after 1800 BC	$33\frac{1}{3}$ (for grain) 20 (for silver)	20 (for grain) $6\frac{1}{4}$ (for silver)	
Mesopotamia-Assyria	1st millennium BC	30–50 (for grain) 20–40 (for silver)		
Mesopotamia-Neo-Babylonia	625–539 BC	20 (for grain) 20 (for silver)	$11\frac{2}{3}$	
Ancient India	Seventh to first century BC	20		60
Ancient Greece	Sixth century BC	16–18		9000 (fourth century BC)
	Second century BC	6–10		
	First century AD	8–9		
Ancient Rome	Fourth century BC	$8\frac{1}{3}$ (for silver)	4	
	First century BC to fourth century AD	12		
Ancient Rome-Egypt	Fifth century BC	100 (for grain) 85 (for silver)		
	Second century BC	5–10		
	Second century AD	6–50		
Ancient Rome-Asia Minor	Second century BC	8–12		
	Second century AD	6–12		

Era		*Normal rates (%)*	*Lower rates (%)*	*Excessive rates (%)*
Ancient Rome-Roman Africa	Second century AD	5–12		
Byzantium	Sixth century	4–8	3	
Medieval Europe	Twelfth century	$43\frac{1}{3}$–120 (England)		
		10–16 (Netherlands) 20 (Genoa)		
	Thirteenth century	5–40		300 (Pawnbrokers)
	Seventeenth century	3–6 (England) 5–$8\frac{1}{3}$(France)		

Source: Homer (1963) and Graeber (2011)

References

Baumol, William. 1990. "Entrepreneurship: Productive, Unproductive and Destructive." *The Journal of Political Economy* 98 (5–1): 893–921.

Böhm-Bawerk, Eugen. 1890. *Capital and Interest: A Critical History of Economical Theory*. London: The Macmillan Company.

Chapra, Muhammad Umer. 1996. *What Is Islamic Economics?* Vol. 9. Islamic Development Bank, Islamic Research and Training Institute.

Chown, John F. 1996. *A History of Money: From AD 800*. London: Routledge.

Conard, Joseph W. 1959. *An Introduction to the Theory of Interest*. Berkeley: University of California Press.

Fisher, Irving. 1930. *The Theory of Interest*. New York: The Macmillan Company.

Geisst, Charles R. 2013. *Beggar Thy Neighbor: A History of Usury and Debt*. University of Pennsylvania Press.

Graeber, David. 2011. *Debt: The First 5000 Years*. New York: Melville House Publishing.

Homer, Sidney. 1963. *A History of Interest Rates*. New Jersey: Rutgers University Press.

"Interest in Merriam-Webster's Dictinonary." 2019. In . https://www.merriam-webster.com/dictionary/interest. Accesed on February 17, 2019.

"Interest in Online Etymology Dictionary." 2019. In . https://www.etymonline.com/word/interest. Accessed on February 17, 2019.

"Interest in Oxford Advanced Learner's Dictionary." 2000. In . New York: Oxford University Press.

Koyama, Mark. 2010. "Evading the Taint of Usury." *Explorations in Economic History* 47 (4).

Küçükkalay, Abdullah Mesud. 2018. *İktisadi Düşüncede Faiz [Interest in Economic Thought]*. Konya: Çizgi Kitabevi.

Medema, Steven G., and Warren J. Samuels, eds. 2003. *The History of Economic Thought: A Reader*. London: Routledge.

Olechnowicz, Cheryl A. 2011. "History of Usury: The Transition of Usury through Ancient Greece, the Rise of Christianity and Islam, and the Expansion of Long-Distance Trade and Capitalism." *Gettysburg Economic Review* 5: 97–109.

Persky, Joseph. 2007. "Retrospectives: From Usury to Interest." *Journal of Economic Perspectives* 21 (1): 227–36.

Schumpeter, Joseph A. 1934. *The Theory of Economic Development*. Cambridge: Harvard University Press.

Smith, Adam. 1776. *The Wealth of Nations*. The Electric Book Co.

Turgot, Anne Robert Jacques. 1766. "Reflections on the Formation and Distribution of Wealth." In *The Turgot Collection*, edited by David Gordon, 5–65. Ludwig von Mises Institute.

Vincent, Joshua. 2014. "Historical, Religious and Scholastic Prohibition of Usury: The Common Origins of Western and Islamic Financial Practices." *Law School Student Scholarship. Paper 600.*

Visser, Wayne AM, and Alastair McIntosh. 1998. "A Short Review of the Historical Critique of Usury." *Accounting, Business & Financial History* 8 (2): 175–89.

CHAPTER 3

Theoretical Development and the Time Preference Theory

The significant role of interest of Interestin lending has always motivated people to think about the nature of interest since ancient times. The philosophers, wise men, religious scholars, and the lawmakers evaluated it economically, morally, and religiously well before modern times. In time, the mobility of money and the need to finance increased further by the development of trade and industry. Besides, the attitude against the legitimacy of interest weakened in Europe by the widening of Protestantism. By the seventeenth century, along with the increased significance of the role of interest in economic life, scholars began to deal with the concept of interest more systematically. The leading mercantilist, physiocrat, and classical economists took part in the pro-interest movement and asserted that interest is legitimate. These economists studied the nature of interest as it was done before. However, this time, the economic aspects of interest, but not religious and moral ones, were in the center of the issue (Küçükkalay 2018). Many theories were developed to explain the causes of the existence of interest and its role in economic activities.

The most cited theories of interest were developed on the concept of *time preference*. As being considered the founder of the modern theory of interest, among others, it must be pointed out that Böhm-Bawerk's approach of time preference has particular importance.

In this chapter, firstly, the basic principles of the significant theories of interest are briefly summarized. In the second section, Böhm-Bawerk's

C. Eyerci, *The Causes and Consequences of Interest Theory*,
https://doi.org/10.1007/978-3-030-78702-8_3

arguments for developing a new theory distinct from the existing ones are presented, and his time preference theory of interest is introduced in more detail. The critiques of Böhm-Bawerk's theory made by various scholars are reviewed in the third section. Lastly, the validity of the theory in the current economic system is evaluated.

3.1 The Theories of Interest

From the beginning, the theory of interest has been studied within the theory of distribution. Accordingly, there are four factors of production in the economy. The workers, landholders, capital owners, and entrepreneurs receive wage, rent, interest, and profit, respectively. However, there have also been some different approaches to the categorization of income. Irving Fisher (1930), for example, asserted that all types of income are interest. Frank H. Knight regarded interest and rent to be the same. As another example, according to Joseph A. Schumpeter (1934), all returns, except the wages, may be considered a form of interest. He defined interest as a deduction from profit like a tax (Conard 1959).

The main question that the theories of interest try to answer is why the lenders of money request and receive payment as interest. There is another question that accompanied the main one: How is the interest rate determined? In general, these two issues have been regarded as separate fields (Conard 1959). However, there were some scholars, like Fisher, who contradicted it. Fisher (1930) claimed that the answer to the second question would also include the answer to the first one.

From another point of view, the main theoretical problem in interest studies is about the causes of interest. The question pursues, almost the same as the abovementioned first question does: Why is there interest? The rest of the problem is about the social and political aspects, and deals with the effects of interest; discusses on the necessity, justice, fairness, usefulness, and goodness of interest; tries to decide whether it should be continued or stopped to use, or modified (Böhm-Bawerk 1890).

Many economists, including most of the classical ones, studied on nonmonetary theories of interest, in which the quantity and velocity of money were not considered in the determination of interest rate. On the contrary, monetary theories were prominent both before and after the classical economists. The reason for the diversity of classical economists might be their more theoretical approach to the issue compared to others.

The pre and postclassical economists were personally involved in the economic activities and administration of the economy more than the classical ones (Conard 1959).

The manner of approaching the issue may be another aspect of the classification of the theories of interest. Böhm-Bawerk (1890), for example, grouped the interest theories as colorless theories, productivity theories, abstinence theories, labor theories, and exploitation theories.

Böhm-Bawerk grouped several economists' assertions on interest under *colorless theories* due to not influencing much on the development of interest theory. He included Turgot, Adam Smith, Ricardo, and McCulloch's works in this group. Smith and some scholars asserted that when interest does not exist, the owner of capital would not be motivated to employ the capital productively. Some others thought that there was no need to explain interest. The alleged causes of interest by some other economists were peculiar and too shallow to be a theory. Although Böhm-Bawerk classified Adam Smith and Ricardo's works in this group and did not regard them as complete interest theories, he stated that the seeds of many later theories were involved in their exertions.

Some of the prominent interest theories, including the ones mentioned above, are briefly reviewed in the following. Although Turgot is noted among the colorless theories by Böhm-Bawerk, his assertion is worth evaluating due to being considered the first scientific approach.

3.1.1 Turgot's Theory of Interest

Anne Robert Jacques Turgot, the French physiocrat, was introduced by Böhm-Bawerk (1890) to be the first scholar who scientifically studied the issue of interest. Turgot defined that lending money at interest was a kind of trade, in which the lender sells the use of money to the borrower. It is the same as renting in that the use of a rented property is sold. Thus, interest is the price of the use of money (Turgot 1766).

When some capital is lent, the lender risks it and loses the income that might be earned by its use during the loan period. On the other hand, the borrower can employ the capital in an investment and make a profit. However, the real causes of the legitimacy of receiving interest are quite different. Since the capital is the lender's own, any capital owner has the right to lend at interest. A lender can do whatever he wants, either keeping the money or lending it by setting conditions or something else. It is just like exchange transactions in which commodities are sold (Turgot

1766). The seller and the lender have the right to request any price for a good and the capital, respectively. Of course, the transaction is possible if a buyer is ready to pay the requested price.

However, lending differs from ordinary exchange transactions about an important issue. An exchange transaction takes place immediately, while a loan transaction is exchanging present money or good against a promise of payment of money or good in the future. In general, the value of the future payment is expected to be higher than the present value of the loan. The borrower pays the increment in addition to the borrowed capital because a lender thinks that "a bird in the hand is better than two in the bush" (p. 215) in Turgot's (1769) words. Such an increment in the value of the loan convinces the lender to lend (Groenewegen 1971).

According to Turgot, the price of the money, namely the interest rate, should be formed in the market like the prices of other commodities. When the number of borrowers increases, demand for money also increases, and the interest rate rises. On the contrary, an increased number of lenders cause an increment in the money supply, and the interest rate falls (Turgot 1766). As being the essential postulate of the classical theory of interest, this mechanism asserts that the interest rate is determined in the market by balancing the demand for capital and the supply of it.

Turgot compared the interest income with incomes from some other investment alternatives. He asserted that the income from lending should be a little higher than the income from land purchased at a price equal to the capital lent. Distinctly, the capital invested in agriculture, industry, and trade should receive higher revenue than the same capital lent at interest (Turgot 1766).

3.1.2 Productivity and Use Theories

Several theories exhibit a common approach regarding the relation of interest with productivity. Scholars including Jean-Baptiste Say, Wilhelm Roscher, Thomas R. Malthus, and Johann von Thünen developed theories that were not wholly the same but commonly asserting that capital had to receive some portion of the income due to being productive (Conard 1959).

The productivity of capital is defined mostly as saving instead of consuming today would help to produce more in the future. An angler using a fishing rod might save some of her income and buy a fisher boat and a net. Thus, she will be able to fish more. Production may be evaluated in two distinct aspects: one in quantity and the other in value. The angler's improvement in production is an example of an increase in quantity (Böhm-Bawerk 1890). On the other hand, the increased price of an aged wine compared to its fresh price is an increase in the value of production (Conard 1959).

The value of the increment in production due to capital usage is expected to be higher than the used capital. Some part of the defined surplus is the yield of capital, and its owner has the right to receive revenue or interest for it. However, Böhm-Bawerk (1890) discussed a case in which the abovementioned expectation not met. When there is no surplus, in other words, when the value of the increased part of the product in quantity is not higher than the capital used, it would not be possible to receive interest.

The use theories, as Böhm-Bawerk named (Conard 1959), seem closely related to the productivity theories. They may be defined to be an extension of productivity theories. However, the use theories, in which F.B.W. von Hermann and Carl Menger's assertions are prominent, differ from the productivity theories by asserting that the use of capital should be considered independently besides the capital itself. The owner of the capital sacrifices both the capital itself and its use by lending it (Böhm-Bawerk 1890). Therefore, the buyer of capital should pay for both the capital itself and its use (Conard 1959).

This time, the value of the increment in production due to capital usage is expected to be higher than the substance of capital used, and the surplus-value is the share that falls to the part of the sacrificed use of capital (Böhm-Bawerk 1890).

3.1.3 Abstinence Theories

Nassau William Senior defined interest as the payment made to the lender for her abstaining from present consumption till the end of the term that capital is lent (Medema and Samuels 2003). Although some others, including Samuel Read, Samuel Bailey, Henri Storch, and George P. Scrope, also developed abstinence theories of interest (Bacon 1992), Senior's theory had been accepted as the most completed classical theory (Bowley 2013).

Senior (2003) defined abstinence as one of the three instruments of production. Others, namely labor and natural agents, are the primary ones. However, abstinence provides the efficiency of labor and natural agents. Abstinence is the action of a capital owner, who abstains from the unproductive use of the capital and prefers a better future production to present output. Abstinence is a source of pain for the capital owner, just like the pain of the labor in production, and interest is the reward that corresponds to the pain. According to Senior, abstinence is also the cause of capital accumulation (Küçükkalay 2018).

Böhm-Bawerk objected to Senior's theory by claiming that abstinence could not be dealt with as an independent production factor. Considering the nature of a production factor, only an entity such as a commodity or a person can provide products. Choosing any of the use of a factor means it has abstained from the use of another one. Then, payment for activity also includes payment for abstinence from alternative activities (Conard 1959).

3.1.4 Labor Theories

Similar to the abstinence theory, the labor theories also defined a distinct production factor. Scholars of labor theories asserted that interest is a legitimate revenue paid for labor, which was previously performed, or its rights were obtained. James Mill, a prominent labor theorist, specifically defined interest as the revenue from stored labor, which is in the form of capital (Conard 1959). Jean G. Courcelle-Seneuil and Albert Schaffle were among the prominent developers of the theory (Böhm-Bawerk 1890).

James Mill (1844) proposed that the cost of production determines the exchange value of a commodity. According to him, there are two productive instruments: labor and capital. Capital is a form of stored labor. Then, the total cost of production is defined by labor alone. Therefore, the determiner of the value of a commodity is labor only.

Böhm-Bawerk (1890) raised a question regarding the distinction between stored labor and current labor. While the present worker is receiving only the current wage, the stored labor, capital, receives more with the addition of interest. What makes the stored labor more valuable or more profitable than the present one? Unless this question finds a satisfying answer, Mill's assertion of the determination of a commodity's value only by labor would be refuted.

3.1.5 Exploitation Theories

The theorists of the exploitation theory asserted that any product is produced by labor alone. However, the workers do not receive the entire revenue from the production due to private property rights, and capital owners take some part of the income. Therefore, interest, which is a part of the value of the product and produced by labor, is obtained by exploiting the needy people (Böhm-Bawerk 1890).

Indeed, measuring the value of a product by the quantity of labor used in its production was an approach that existed since Adam Smith and Ricardo. As it was, facing such a question was not surprising: If the producer of the value is labor, why does it not receive all the revenue? The only plausible explanation was that the capital owners, a class of society, take some part of the value produced by the workers alone, as parasites do. Scholars, including the two prominent ones, Karl Rodbertus and Karl Marx, studied the problem within the mentioned framework.

Böhm-Bawerk attempted to refute the Marxian approach in two aspects (Conard 1959). He denied Marx's assertion that the use-value does not have any impact on the exchange of goods. Since the utility received from a product determines its use-value, and use-value determines its exchange value, the quantity of labor used in production does not have a direct impact on the formation of exchange value.

Secondly, Böhm-Bawerk asked whether the labor should receive all the returns, even when the entire value is not produced by itself. According to him, labor deserves all income from its products, but it does not always make the production alone. The revenue can be the current value of a product and received now, or the future value and received in the future. However, Rodbertus and other socialists claimed that the laborer should receive the entire future value of the product now (Böhm-Bawerk 1890). Böhm-Bawerk focused on the difference between his and the exploitation theorists' approaches. He asserted that payment made to labor now for a product, which will be ready in the future, has to be different from the value of the product when sold. The value of the product may increase during the time between the labor payment and sale. Others may receive the increment, and it is not the exploitation of labor. The cause of the increment in value is the essential research issue of the theory of interest (Conard 1959).

3.1.6 Impatience Theory

The Impatience Theory of interest is similar to the time preference theory of Böhm-Bawerk. However, they have two essential differences. Irving Fisher, the founder of the Impatience Theory, did not agree with Böhm-Bawerk about the distinction he made between land and capital. He also objected to Böhm-Bawerk's assertion of the technical superiority of present goods over future goods as a cause of time preference (Seager 1912).

Fisher (1930) defined the rate of interest as the price in the exchange of present goods with future goods. While two goods are exchanged at a *price rate*, a good at present is exchanged against the same good in the future at *an interest rate*. It has to be pointed out that the rate of interest is partly subjective due to the marginal preference of present goods to future goods. Fisher named it as time preference or human impatience.

The theory claims that the degree of impatience is closely related to the size, distribution in time, composition, and certainty of the expected income. Regarding the concept of marginal preference, the theory also asserts that the personal characteristic is another determinant of the degree of impatience (Fisher 1930).

However, some other factors are also effective in the formation of impatience. Fisher (1930) asserted that market rules and investment opportunities have implications on the degree of impatience.

Thus, the degree of impatience, in other words, the interest rate, has various determinants. These determinants are not stable in time, and some of them are not directly related to economic factors. In Fisher's (1930) words: "Any causes tending to affect intelligence, foresight, self-control, habits, the longevity of man, family affection, and fashion will have their influence upon the rate of interest" (p. 305). By presenting the factors in the formation of interest, Fisher (1930) stated that the real interest rate is almost not negative. It is possible in theory, but in practice, the necessary conditions never met.

3.1.7 Loanable Funds Theory

The Loanable Funds Theory, also known as the Neoclassical Theory of Interest, was developed by Dennis Robertson, Bertil Ohlin, and others. Ohlin (1937) denied the previous classical approach that the rate of interest is determined by the balance of the demand for and supply of savings. He did also not agree with the idea that the rate of interest balances the planned savings and planned investments. He stated that, since the interest rate is the price of a loan, it is determined by the demand for and supply of lendable funds.

The theory does not imply the existence of one single interest rate determined for all types of loans. Regarding its risk and maturity, each loan may have specific demand and supply, and the revenue may differ. The theory defines the demand for and supply of loans, not as stock quantities only. The demand and supply may be treated as stock quantities at a particular time or as flow quantities for a period (Conard 1959).

3.1.8 Liquidity Preference Theory

John Maynard Keynes (2013)stated that an individual constructs her time preference by deciding how much of her income will be consumed or saved for future needs. The decision of the form of saving is the next stage. Will the saving totally or partly be in liquid form that can be used immediately? Keynes defined liquidity preference as part of the savings kept as money or equivalent.

According to Keynes, the common mistake made in the previous theories of interest was not considering the liquidity preference. Saving or waiting could not be the source of interest. The determiner of the interest rate is the liquidity preference of an individual that the more an individual consent not to keep her savings liquid, the higher the revenue of interest will be.

On the other hand, the quantity of money also has a role in the determination of the interest rate. It is so because when the interest rate decreases, people tend to hold more cash, but when it increases, the desire to hold cash decreases and a cash surplus emerges (Keynes 2013).

3.1.9 Pure Time Preference Theory

The Pure Time Preference theory of interest is developed by Frank A. Fetter (1914), who was introduced by Rothbard (1977) as the first economist to define time preference as the mere cause of interest. The theory that was extended by Ludwig von Mises (2006) and Murray N. Rothbard (Potuzak 2016a) states that the cause of the existence of interest is the significant prevalence of positive time preference. Although

Fetter recognized the validity of both positive and negative time preference, Mises asserted that positive time preference is the mere possible attitude due to the human nature that people want to meet all demands as soon as possible (Rothbard 2011). The only motivation for practicing interest is people's preference for sooner goods and services rather than later ones, and there is no place for productivity in explaining the concept of interest (Kirzner 2011).

Mises (2006) clearly defined time preference as a necessity of human action, namely an essential part of human nature. According to him, grounding time preference on psychological explanations, what Böhm-Bawerk did, was a big mistake. Such justification could not provide the general acceptance of time preference. It is so because a universal rule has not to be based on psychological evidence, while psychology can explain some, or maybe many, persons' attitudes.

The prominent founders and basic principles of the reviewed interest theories are summarized in Table 3.1.

3.2 Böhm-Bawerk's Time Preference Theory

Eugen von Böhm-Bawerk, the founder of the modern theory of interest (Conard 1959; Potuzak 2016b), criticized several previous interest theories (Böhm-Bawerk 1890, 1903) and developed a new one based on time preference (Böhm-Bawerk 1930). He described time preference as the origin of the legitimacy of the existence of interest.

A capital owner was receiving a perpetual income from capital without making any effort, and Böhm-Bawerk asserted that defining the reason for such an income would help to find the cause of the existence of interest. The main theoretical problem was finding the answer to the question: Why is there interest? The social and political factors such as the necessity, justice, fairness, usefulness, and goodness of interest were secondary issues. The decision of whether permitting or controlling interest or the mechanism of formation of the interest rate was not relevant to the cause of the existence of interest but about its effects (Böhm-Bawerk 1890).

3.2.1 The Theoretical, Social and Political Aspects of Interest

Interest, as an economic issue, has to be studied in many aspects, including its theoretical, social, and political problems. In this context, the distinction made between the theoretical and other problems was not only

Table 3.1 Some theories of interest, their founders and basic principles

Theory	*Prominent founders*	*Basic principle*
Turgot's theory	Anne Robert Jacques Turgot	Interest rate is determined in the market by balancing the demand for capital and the supply of it
Productivity theories	Jean-Baptiste Say, Wilhelm Roscher, Thomas R. Malthus, Johann von Thünen	Capital has to receive some portion of the income due to being productive
Use theories	F. B. W. von Hermann, Carl Menger	The borrower should pay for both the capital itself and its use
Abstinence theories	Nassau William Senior, Samuel Read, Samuel Bailey, Henri Storch, George P. Scrope	Abstinence is a source of pain for the capital owner, just like the pain of the labor in production, and interest is the reward that corresponds to the pain
Labor theories	James Mill, Jean G. Courcelle-Seneuil, Albert Schaffle	Interest is a legitimate revenue paid for labor, which was previously performed
Exploitation theories	Karl Rodbertus, Karl Marx	Interest, which is a part of the value of the product and produced by labor, is obtained by exploiting the needy people
Impatience Theory	Irving Fisher	Interest is partly subjective due to the marginal preference of present goods, which depends on human impatience
Böhm-Bawerk's time preference theory	Eugen von Böhm-Bawerk	The cause of the existence of interest is the difference between the present and future values that people attribute
Loanable Funds Theory	Dennis Robertson, Bertil Ohlin	Interest rate is determined by the demand for and supply of loan funds
Liquidity Preference Theory	John Maynard Keynes	Interest rate is determined by the liquidity preference, which is defined as the part of savings kept as money or equivalent

(continued)

Table 3.1 (continued)

Theory	*Prominent founders*	*Basic principle*
Pure Time Preference Theory	Frank A. Fetter, Ludwig von Mises, Murray N. Rothbard	The mere cause of the existence of interest is people's preference for sooner goods and services rather than later ones

for methodological purposes. Böhm-Bawerk (1890) defined the answer to the theoretical question to be positive with the statement of "To the question as to the causes of interest there can be only one answer and its truth everyone must recognize if the laws of thought are correctly applied" (p. 2). Besides, the answers to the social and political questions were normative. He overemphasized the importance of distinguishing the theoretical features of the issue from its social and political aspects. These two groups of problems are closely related. By being well informed of the causes of interest, any normative conclusion can be successfully drawn. However, according to him, a scientific approach requires working on the theoretical problem and the rest, separately. Taking these two distinct issues together would prevent finding the right answers to the questions, in neither positive nor normative domain. The normative evaluations are being naturally determined by the beliefs, wishes, passions, and predispositions. In the case of studying the normative and positive issues together, the theoretical part of the work would be guided by the abovementioned normative determinants. Conversely, the theoretical considerations may wrongly guide the evaluations on the effects of interest.

As an example, when the two problems are not worked on distinctly, an observation of an increment in production in an interest-existed environment may lead to a thought that the cause of interest is the productivity of capital. Similarly, considering the competition of labor with capital, it may be thought that interest is yielding from the exploitation of the laborer. Observation of the good or bad results of practicing interest does not help to understand the cause of the existence of interest (Böhm-Bawerk 1890).

Böhm-Bawerk (1890) asserted that due to not considering the importance of working on the positive and normative issues separately, many economists made mistakes in their works on the theory of interest. He claimed that none of the interest theories developed up to his time rightly answered the question on the cause of interest. After reviewing and criticizing many interest theories, he asked once more:"What really is the problem of interest?" (p. 421).

3.2.2 *Superiority of Present Goods to Future Goods*

Four years after the publication of Capital and Interest (Böhm-Bawerk 1890), Böhm-Bawerk (1930) presented his theory of interest in The Positive Theory of Capital in 1888. *Time preference* was in the center of Böhm-Bawerk's (1930) theory. It was defined as *people's attribution of more value to present goods than future goods with the same quality and quantity.*

The future goods, namely the goods and services consumed in the future, are being produced, valued, bought, and sold, just like the present goods. Considering its role in the formation of time preference, the mechanism of the valuation of future goods deserves special attention. There is no doubt that all goods are valued to the extent of the marginal utility they provide, and it is so for future ones. However, there is a single distinction. Since the future is uncertain, future goods are valued a little, sometimes farther, under the future value of the marginal utility provided by them (Böhm-Bawerk 1930).

Böhm-Bawerk (1930) introduced three main reasons, which are presented in the following, for the valuation of present goods higher than future ones.

3.2.2.1 *Expectation of a Lower Marginal Utility in the Future*

The difference between the needs for present and future goods is one of the determinants of the valuation of present goods higher than future ones. The difference in requirements may have various reasons. People that have temporary problems may prefer to have goods at present by expecting to meet their urgent needs. Similarly, some others, such as young professionals, may assume to have higher income in the future and prefer present goods to future ones. Then, it is possible to assert that the marginal utility of a good at present is higher than its marginal utility in the future for both groups.

On the other hand, there are some different cases in which people may worry about facing unexpected problems in the future, or may think that their income will be lower, e.g., after retirement. As might be expected, such individuals store durable goods or save money for the future. However, the attitude of valuing present goods higher, namely the superiority of present goods, is not affected only by the concerns of future needs. While future goods can be consumed only in the future, present goods are available to consume both now and in the future (Böhm-Bawerk 1930).

3.2.2.2 *Underestimation of the Future*

The common attitude of the underestimation of the future is another reason for the valuation of present goods higher than future goods. Not only the pleasures but also the pains of the future are less important than the present pleasures and pains. Most of the people, more or less, underestimate the future. Although they are aware of the causes of many future health problems, people do not avoid unhealthy foods or give up smoking. Similarly, it is widely experienced that most people tend to postpone their planned tasks to the times closer to deadlines. For example, students may not uniformly distribute their exertion to the prescribed term; instead, they work little at the beginning and hardly complete their task by overexertion towards the end. Actually, in such cases, received present pleasure is worth far less than the future pain.

Underestimation of the future is justified in the field of psychology. The first of the three causes that guide people to underestimate the future is the imperfectness of the prediction of future desires. The imperfect imagination reduces the influence of some wants on the valuation of future goods, and it causes the marginal utility of future goods to be low. The second cause is the lack of will. Although they are aware of the consequences of their present decisions, most of the people cannot behave with a strong will that is appropriate to the real value of the future. The last cause is simply the finiteness and uncertainty of life. There is always a possibility of not living up to a planned future. Moreover, the future is uncertain and may not be as it is expected today (Böhm-Bawerk 1930). Then, thinking along with the idiom: *tomorrow will take care of itself*, causes the underestimation of the future.

3.2.2.3 *Technical Superiority of Present Goods in Production*

The savings, namely capital, helps to produce more in the future. However, the superiority of present goods is not just the result of the physical productivity of capital. Production takes time, and by use of the same productive instruments, the process that takes more time yields more compared to the process that takes less time. Then, the earlier possessed goods may be employed in longer production processes in which the production is more not only in quantity but also in value. The availability of using for longer production processes makes present goods technically superior to future goods.

The former two reasons are about the preference of the present goods for current consumption. In a case relevant to the third reason, the present goods are preferred for more products in value in the future rather than consuming at present. Although the first two reasons may be influential cumulatively for an individual, the third reason does not exist with the first two ones concurrently. An individual has to decide to consume a good now or employ it in production, expecting more in the future (Böhm-Bawerk 1930).

The causes of the preference of the present goods that Böhm-Bawerk asserted are illustrated in Fig. 3.1.

3.2.3 Time Preference and Interest

Böhm-Bawerk (1930) asserted that the cause of the existence of interest is the difference between the present and future values that people attribute to the same good.

The difference is apparent in the loan process in which present goods are exchanged for future ones. However, loans do not always bear interest. Interest-free lending is similar to selling commodities under the market price and is made to specific groups due to personal reasons such as charity and friendship.

The superiority of present goods is not influential only on the formation of interest in lending. A more complex role appears in defining the profit of the capital owner's entrepreneurship. An entrepreneur buys machines, raw material, use of land and labor, manages the production process (Böhm-Bawerk 1930), may also work personally, and supervise the process intellectually (Böhm-Bawerk 1890). The production makes gain that is called profit, surplus value, or natural interest on capital.

The complexity is about defining the source of this gain. The gain is the surplus of the value of the product over the cost of production. However, production takes time, forming a lag between the time of cost and the time of outcome. Then, the future price of a product that is not ready yet has to be paid today by the use of previously saved capital. The question here is whether all the profit yields from the capital. If not, some

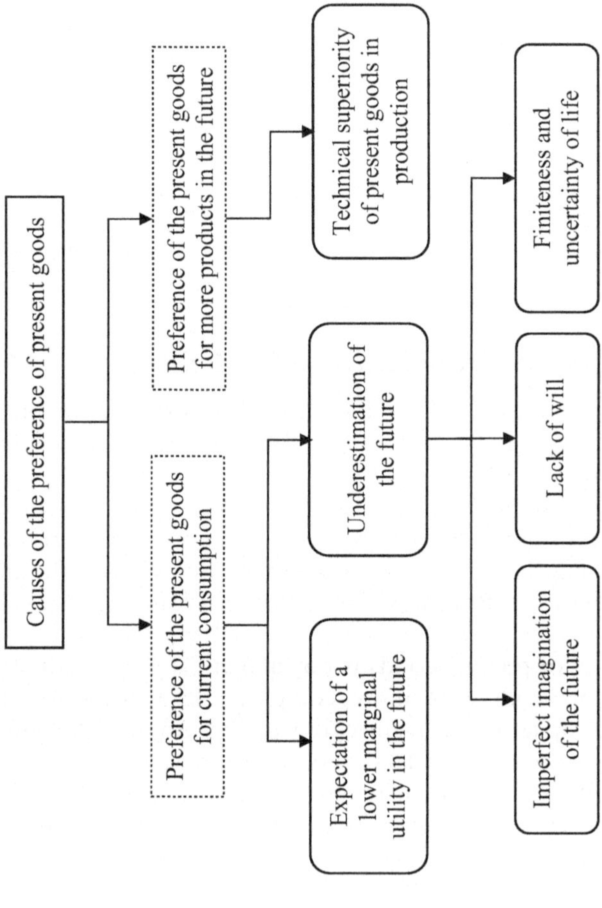

Fig. 3.1 Böhm-Bawerk's causes of the superiority of present goods to future goods

part of the return may bear from the entrepreneur's will and initiative. An approach in answering the question advises calculating the capital's share as if it was lent in the market at an interest rate of a safe loan. The remainder of the profit is the entrepreneur's share. However, some others consider such a sharing to be unreasonable due to the homogeneity of profit (Böhm-Bawerk 1890).

The implication of time preference in the labor market is a little different. Since production takes time, payment to the labor is made in advance by previous savings in most of the production processes. Whoever the employer is, an own-account worker or an entrepreneur employing others, some capital has to be used for either self-subsistence or wages of hired workers, until the completion of the product. The present value of labor, the payment made to the employees today, is naturally under the future value of the completed product. This fact enables the formation of a surplus value (Böhm-Bawerk 1930).

3.3 Critiques of Böhm-Bawerk's Theory of Interest

Since Böhm-Bawerk was regarded as the founder of the modern theory of interest, many scholars studied the issue by considering his assertion. There were scholars both agreed with and opposed to Böhm-Bawerk's approach. Some of the critiques of Böhm-Bawerk's theory were raised when he was alive, and he found the chance to respond (Böhm-Bawerk 1895a, 1895b, 1896).

Francis A. Walker (1892) was one of the first scholars that raised some issues against Böhm-Bawerk's theory and criticized his method of evaluation of the old assertions. He objected to the approach that labor and land were the two main production factors, while capital was a factor derived from others. He emphasized the fact that the capital's role in the existence of interest would not change, whether it is an essential production factor or not. Böhm-Bawerk (1895b)agreed with Walker but reminded that his work was about not only the source of interest but also the origin of capital.

A more significant criticism was on Böhm-Bawerk's fundamental principle of the people's undervaluation of the future compared to the present. Walker (1892) asserted that a community, with members widely undervaluing the future goods, would not grow and be weaker because any opportunity such as usurious borrowing would be used to consume at present. According to him, the cause of the existence of interest on capital is explained by the productivity theory of interest: it is the productivity of capital.

Walker, finally, pointed out his disagreement with Böhm-Bawerk's one-sided conception of the source of the value. Although he accused Böhm-Bawerk of claiming that value is determined on the side of consumption only, Böhm-Bawerk (1895b) refuted it and explained how production does not determine the value alone, but the market, wherein the producer faces with the consumer, does it.

John B. Clark (1894) opposed to the conception of people's attribution of more value to present goods than future goods with the same quality and quantity. The objection was to the assumption of the sameness of present and future goods. He asserted that for the conception to be valid, such a comparison should be made in all aspects, but the capital owners cannot do it. Instead, it may be possible to compare the present *true capital* with that of the future. Since true capital is defined as the amount of productive wealth, its valuation is easier than valuing concrete capital goods. Böhm-Bawerk (1895a) accepted that he had mistaken in merely mentioning concrete capital goods that were supposed to be identical with true capital. Indeed, Clark's elaboration was nothing short of Böhm-Bawerk's intention.

This time, after declaring that he agreed with Böhm-Bawerk on the nature of the capital owner's behavior, Clark (1895)reviewed Böhm-Bawerk's (1895a) example of money as capital to be compared. He reminded that the thing to be measured should be a subjective value, and asserted that comparing present money itself with future money would not serve the purpose. Actually, according to him, the compared thing is not money but the sum of wealth, which is connected to money.

The critiques of Böhm-Bawerk's theory mostly focused on his approach in explaining the technical superiority of present goods in production as a cause of interest (Murphy 2003). Frank A. Fetter accused Böhm-Bawerk of contradictions, such as turning back to productivity theory after demolishing the old productivity theories (Fetter 1902).Fetter asserted that interest would emerge as long as a future service exists notwithstanding the absence of a production process, and presenting the roundabout process as a cause of interest makes the theory a productivity theory of interest. However, Robert P. Murphy (2003) refused the accusation of the contradictions in Böhm-Bawerk's approach and claimed that Böhm-Bawerk did not change his opinion from a solely time preference-based interest conception to a productivity-based interest conception. Indeed, he described interest as an income based on the valuation of present goods higher than future goods and defined the technical superiority of present goods by roundabout processes as one of the causes of interest.

Fisher (1907) also objected to the role of the technical superiority of present goods in production. He disagreed with Böhm-Bawerk's assertion that the first two reasons (the expectation of a lower marginal utility in the future and underestimation of the future) of interest cannot be active with the third one (the technical superiority of present goods in production) concurrently. He claimed that the effectiveness of the third cause depends on the existence of any of the first two causes. When others do not exist, the technical superiority of present goods cannot produce interest alone.

Although he accepted the productivity of some time-consuming or roundabout operations, Keynes (2013) presented less time-consuming processes, in which the production is more. For example, a short but dangerous process may produce more than a long but safe one. Such a consideration may be regarded to be needless, because, although not explicitly emphasized by Böhm-Bawerk, the processes compared in his work were assumed almost the same in all aspects except the lengths of production time.

Mises (2006) noted that Böhm-Bawerk was the first to make an accurate explanation of the problem correcting the mistakes of the productivity theories of interest, and was also the first to stress the role of the time taken in production. However, he claimed that Böhm-Bawerk had fallacies in factually interpreting the problem of interest. According to Mises, a significant fallacy is about grounding time preference on psychological explanations. Such a justification is not satisfactory for a general acceptance of time preference, because, since psychology can explain some, or maybe many, persons' attitudes, a universal rule has not to be based on any psychological evidence. Secondly, he asserted that Böhm-Bawerk's approach to the time-consuming characteristic of production did not allow him entirely to avoid overestimating the role of productivity in time preference, although he previously refuted.

It is observed that the critiques of Böhm-Bawerk's theory center on its defining a sort of productivity theory, which he confuted before, by asserting the technical superiority of the present goods in the roundabout processes. Besides, the undervaluation of future goods is also opposed in a few aspects.

Firstly, such an attitude has the risk of guiding people to usurious borrowing for present consumption. Undoubtedly, it is the case for some individuals. However, each individual underestimates the future to an extent, and most of them can make an implicit evaluation of the level of the preference of present goods, rationally. Secondly, psychology cannot explain each individual's attitude, and any psychological explanation is not appropriate to explain the cause of interest as a universal rule. Finally, the first two causes related to the preference of present consumption, and the third one, which is about preferring more products in the future, are not effective concurrently. It is right that although the first two causes may be influential cumulatively, an individual has to decide to consume a good now or employ it in production, expecting more in the future, as it is stated within the theory.

3.4 The Validity of Böhm-Bawerk's Theory in Present Economic System

Böhm-Bawerk's time preference theory of interest is still a subject of study for scholars more than a hundred years after its assertion. There were many other interest theories developed after Böhm-Bawerk such as Fisher's (1930) Impatience Theory; Fetter (1914), Mises (2006), and Rothbard's (2011) Pure Time Preference Theory; Keynes' (2013) liquidity preference theory; Robertson, Ohlin (1937) and others' Loanable Funds Theory; and Knight and Schumpeter's theories. Some of these theories, such as Impatience Theory and Pure Time Preference Theory, are based on closely similar concepts with Böhm-Bawerk's theory.

Even at the beginning of the 1980s, Böhm-Bawerk's description of the concept of positive time preference was considered the clearest one up to time (Olson and Bailey 1981). However, as it is briefly reviewed in the previous section, Böhm-Bawerk's theory was criticized from various aspects, particularly for the asserted third cause of interest, the technical superiority of present goods in production. Murphy (2003) attempted to refute the claims by responding to the major critics and contributed to the survival of Böhm-Bawerk's theory of interest.

On the other hand, Jörg Guido Hülsmann (2002) asserted a new theory of interest that is built on Böhm-Bawerk's conception but claimed that his approach used realist cases originated from human action, rather than imaginary fictions.

The causes of interest presented by Böhm-Bawerk have been studied in various works. The *discount factor*, a widely used ratio in present economic analysis and models referring to the intertemporal marginal rate of substitution, was defined as a measure of *time preference* and *impatience*. The relation between the discount factor and the lack of imagination of the future was evaluated (Becker and Mulligan 1997).

It was found by another model-based work that the interest rate is jointly determined by Böhm-Bawerk's real and Keynes' monetary causes. The result implies that Böhm-Bawerk's theory of interest is consistent with Keynes' theory. More significantly, the scholars observed the reasons for the existence of interest asserted by Böhm-Bawerk are still valid in economic theory (Van Suntum and Neugebauer 2014).

The emergence of negative real interest rates in developed countries raised another question on Böhm-Bawerk's theory regarding the nature of positive time preference used in explaining the cause of a positive interest rate. A discounted utility model (Frederick et al. 2002) was used to evaluate the convenience of Böhm-Bawerk's theory to the new situation, and it was observed that it could explain the case of the negative interest rate. In particular, Böhm-Bawerk's first cause of interest, the difference between the present and future marginal utilities, is the best in explaining the case.

Böhm-Bawerk's third cause, the technical superiority of present goods in production, is also significant in the explanation of the negative interest rate situation. When capital is misallocated or consumed, productivity is adversely affected. The failure in allocation or diminishing of capital is somehow related to the recession of the economy in which the interest rate may be very low or negative (Potuzak 2016b). However, it has to be noted that such a meltdown of capital that is affecting productivity is not a case of a usual situation but may emerge under an unusual condition of a recession.

References

Bacon, Charley Arthur. 1992. "The Abstinence Theory of Nassau Senior and Its Critique by Eugen Von Bohm Bawerk." Master of Science, Iowa State University, Department of Economics.

Becker, Gary S., and Casey B. Mulligan. 1997. "The Endogenous Determination of Time Preference." *The Quarterly Journal of Economics* 112 (3): 729–58.

Böhm-Bawerk, Eugen. 1890. *Capital and Interest: A Critical History of Economical Theory*. London: Macmillan.
———. 1895a. "The Positive Theory of Capital and Its Critics-I." *The Quarterly Journal of Economics* 9 (2): 113–31.
———. 1895b. "The Positive Theory of Capital and Its Critics-II." *The Quarterly Journal of Economics* 9 (3): 235–56.
———. 1896. "The Positive Theory of Capital and Its Critics-III." *The Quarterly Journal of Economics* 10 (2): 121–55.
———. 1903. *Recent Literature on Interest (1884–1899): A Supplement to "Capital and Interest."* New York: Macmillan.
———. 1930. *The Positive Theory of Capital*. New York: G.E.Stechert.
Bowley, Marian. 2013. *Nassau Senior and Classical Economics*. London: Routledge.
Clark, John B. 1894. "The Genesis of Capital." *Hand Book of the American Economic Association* 9 (1): 64–68.
———. 1895. "The Origin of Interest." *The Quarterly Journal of Economics* 9 (3): 257–78.
Conard, Joseph W. 1959. *An Introduction to the Theory of Interest*. Berkeley: University of California Press.
Fetter, Frank Albert. 1902. "The 'Roundabout Process' in the Interest Theory." *The Quarterly Journal of Economics* 17 (1): 163–80.
———. 1914. "Interest Theories, Old and New." *The American Economic Review* 4 (1): 68–92.
Fisher, Irving. 1907. *The Rate of Interest*. New York: Macmillan.
———. 1930. *The Theory of Interest*. New York: Macmillan.
Frederick, Shane, George Loewenstein, and Ted O'donoghue. 2002. "Time Discounting and Time Preference: A Critical Review." *Journal of Economic Literature* 40 (2): 351–401.
Groenewegen, Peter Diderik. 1971. "A Re-Interpretation of Turgot's Theory of Capital and Interest." *The Economic Journal* 81 (322): 327–40.
Hülsmann, Jörg Guido. 2002. "A Theory of Interest." *Quarterly Journal of Austrian Economics* 5 (4): 77–110.
Keynes, John Maynard. 2013. *The Collected Writings of John Maynard Keynes-The General Theory of Employment, Interest and Money*, vol. VII. New York: Cambridge University Press.
Kirzner, Israel M. 2011. "The Pure Time-Preference Theory of Interest: An Attempt at Clarification." In *The Pure Time-Preference Theory of Interest*, edited by Jeffrey M. Herbener, 99–126. Ludwig von Mises Institute.
Küçükkalay, Abdullah Mesud. 2018. *İktisadi Düşüncede Faiz [Interest in Economic Thought]*. Konya: Çizgi Kitabevi.
Medema, Steven G., and Warren J. Samuels, eds. 2003. *The History of Economic Thought: A Reader*. London: Routledge.

Mill, James. 1844. *Elements of Political Economy*. London: Henry G. Bohn.

Mises, Ludwig von. 2006. *Human Action: A Treatise on Economics*. Indianapolis: Liberty Fund.

Murphy, Robert P. 2003. "Unanticipated Intertemporal Change in Theories of Interest." New York: New York University, Graduate School of Arts and Science.

Ohlin, Bertil. 1937. "Some Notes on the Stockholm Theory of Savings and Investments II." *The Economic Journal* 47 (186): 221–40.

Olson, Mancur, and Martin J. Bailey. 1981. "Positive Time Preference." *Journal of Political Economy* 89 (1): 1–25.

Potuzak, Pavel. 2016a. "The Pure Time Preference Theory: A Neoclassical Critique." Available at SSRN 2868789. https://ssrn.com/abstract=2868789.

———. 2016b. "What Can We Learn from the Böhm-Bawerkian Theory in the World of Zero Interest?" Available at SSRN 2865082. https://ssrn.com/abstract=2865082.

Rothbard, Murray N., ed. 1977. "Introduction." In *Capital, Interest, and Rent: Essays in the Theory of Distribution by Frank A. Fetter*, 1–24. Kansas City: Sheed Andrews and McMeel.

———. 2011. "Time Preference." In *The Pure Time-Preference Theory of Interest*, edited by Jeffrey M. Herbener, 59–66. Ludwig von Mises Institute.

Schumpeter, Joseph A. 1934. *The Theory of Economic Development*. Cambridge: Harvard University Press.

Seager, Henry R. 1912. "The Impatience Theory of Interest." *The American Economic Review* 2 (4): 834–51.

Senior, Nassau William. 2003. "An Outline of the Science of Political Economy." In *The History of Economic Thought: A Reader*, edited by Steven G. Medema and Warren J. Samuels. London: Routledge.

Turgot, Anne Robert Jacques. 1766. "Reflections on the Formation and Distribution of Wealth." In *The Turgot Collection*, edited by David Gordon, 5–65. Ludwig von Mises Institute.

———. 1769. "Extracts from 'Paper on Lending at Interest.'" In *The Turgot Collection*, edited by David Gordon, 205–21. Ludwig von Mises Institute.

Van Suntum, Ulrich, and Tom Neugebauer. 2014. "Böhm-Bawerk Meets Keynes: What Does Determine the Interest Rate, and Can It Become Negative?" *University of Münster, Center of Applied Economic Research Münster Discussion Paper* 65: 127–45.

Walker, Francis A. 1892. "Dr. Boehm-Bawerk's Theory of Interest." *Quarterly Journal of Economics* 6: 399–416.

CHAPTER 4

The Motivation for Controlling Interest and Its Instruments

Long before the efforts to understand and explain the causes of interest, probably as old as the existence of interest itself, a debate had emerged on its legitimacy. Since ancient times, many societies have condemned interest, and administrative and religious authorities have regulated the practice of interest by either limiting its rate or prohibiting it wholly.

There were various upper limits defined for interest rate, changing in time by type of loan, lender, and borrower, in Sumer, Babylonia, Assyria, ancient India, ancient Greece, ancient Rome, Eastern Roman Empire, and Medieval Europe. There were also some periods in ancient Greece and ancient Rome, during which all the types of interest-bearing activities were prohibited (Homer 1963; Visser and McIntosh 1998; Graeber 2011; Olechnowicz 2011).

From the beginning, religions have had considerable influences on the existence of interest-bearing practices. Hinduism and Buddhism regulated interest-based lending, while Christianity and Islam banned it. Unlike them, although forbidding interest-based transactions among Jews, Judaism allowed its believers to lend non-Jews at interest (Visser and McIntosh 1998). However, in Christian practice, first the Protestant authorities, then the Catholic Church removed the prohibition gradually and allowed people to receive interest up to a defined limit that is tolerable (Chown 1996; Visser and McIntosh 1998). The Church's decree of the acceptable rate does not influence much the Christian world,

C. Eyerci, *The Causes and Consequences of Interest Theory*,
https://doi.org/10.1007/978-3-030-78702-8_4

including Europe, today. However, there are still legally defined limits on interest rates of various types of loans and transactions in many countries (Coco and De Meza 2009), including most of the states of United States (Homer 1963; Lewison 1999) and almost all members of the European Union (Reifner et al. 2010).

In the first section of this chapter, the reasons for prohibiting interest or limiting its rate, arising from various motivations, are presented. The legal, financial, religious, and ethical instruments used in the regulation of interest rates are briefly introduced in the second section.

4.1 The Motivation for Prohibiting and Limiting Interest

The abovementioned and many other probable arrangements had been made for various reasons such as belief, ethics, or protection of the needy. The regulations were not only based on the legal ground but also religion, and ethical enforcements were in use (Visser and McIntosh 1998).

The regulations made for limitation and prohibition of interest in history and today as well arose from many common concerns and claims. According to the regulation supporters, there are many reasons for being against interest. The asserted common reasons are:

- Interest is an income received without working,
- It is benefiting from the poor people,
- It is a cause of economic instability,
- It is double billing,
- It is discounting the future (Visser and McIntosh 1998),
- It is a cause of wealth transfer from borrowers to lenders (Rougeau 1996),
- It is enhancing the inequality in the distribution of wealth (Visser and McIntosh 1998),
- It decreases the tendency to entrepreneurship (Sharawy 2000), and its high rate restrains investment,
- It inspires people selfishness, inhumanity, and avarice (Farooq 2012),
- It guides people to laziness (Khan 2013),
- It causes a problem of unequal bargaining power,
- It overburdens consumers with debt,
- It is unfair at high rates (Durkin 1993),

- It causes a form of slavery (Erdem 2018),
- It undermines the spirituality of people (DeLorenzo 2006) and makes them more secular,
- It transforms money into a purpose itself rather than being a medium of exchange.

Some of the more economics-related claims of these are briefly elaborated below.

4.1.1 An Income Without Working

Working is considered the counterpart of being able to live. To afford living expenses, one is expected to work. In this regard, interest was considered as an income received without working, by various religious, political, social, and ethical thoughts. The Church defined interest as the return of a barren source received without working and taking any risk. As Aristotle asserted in ancient Greece (Visser and McIntosh 1998), living without working is considered unnatural.

A similar approach was raised by Islam and defined the fixed interest to be different from trade in which a non-guaranteed profit is gained by initiative and working (Visser and McIntosh 1998). Interest is prohibited because the wealth gathered from interest-bearing activities is not based on working (Sharawy 2000), and this contradicts the principle of working and productivity of Islam (Choudhury and Malik 1992).

From this general perspective, it must be mentioned that the meaning of *working* is not clear enough. In modern economic literature, working is a wide-range concept that includes using all kinds of human physical efforts and mental abilities, such as planning, advising, forecasting, arranging, managing, etc.

4.1.2 Benefiting from the Poor People

The needy people usually borrow for consumption, and charging interest to needy people for the loans prevents them from getting better. Although poor people use the loans for financing their daily necessities rather than luxury goods, they pay more interest than others do (Caskey 1994; Visser and McIntosh 1998). It is so because the poor people, who do not have any other alternative, are borrowing at higher interest rates due to being riskier for the lenders (Lewison 1999).

Although not widely accepted, a marginal Islamic view on interest asserted that the forbidden riba is only the interest on loans borrowed for consumption purposes (Visser and McIntosh 1998). Such an approach might aim to protect the poor people from exploitive effects of interest by forbidding interest-based loans for consumption purposes while allowing lending for productive purposes.

An objection to interest, regarding its exploitive character, was raised by the theorists of the exploitation theory. According to them, although labor is the only production factor, the workers share the income received from production with capital owners. Paying interest, a part of the value of the product produced by labor, to the capital owner is the exploitation of the needy people (Böhm-Bawerk 1890).

4.1.3 Enhancing the Inequality in Distribution of Wealth

A common idea of interest claims that it makes the rich richer and the poor poorer. The lender, who is the owner of the capital, uses her wealth to get more, causing an unfair distribution of wealth (Shahar et al. 2016). A recent example of the case is from Germany. In 1982, each of the 10% of German households with the highest income had net interest revenue of 34,200 Marks. In the same year, each of the 10% of households with the lowest income paid 1,800 Marks in net as interest. The total net interest payment of each household in the group of 80% of households with lower income was 35,900 Marks. In other words, the interest revenue of 2.5 million highest-income households was paid by the 20 million lower-income households (Kennedy 1995).

An argument supporting this approach asserts that the existence of interest reduces the total utility of society. Since the marginal utility of the rich people is less than the marginal utility of the poor on average, the utility gained from the received interest by the rich lenders is far less than the utility lost for the paid interest by the poor borrowers. Thus, the mechanism that transfers wealth from the poor to the rich causes the total utility to decrease. Unless it is proved that the interest-based transactions are economically efficient and increase the overall utility, interest will be accused of promoting tyranny (Visser and McIntosh 1998).

The argued wealth transfer from the poor to the rich is also one of the reasons of Islam for prohibiting interest. Such a transfer causes the accumulation of wealth and political power in the hands of a group, and this violates the principle of distributive equity (Choudhury and Malik 1992).

A different approach objecting to interest claims that the accumulation of capital due to the existence of interest-based transactions would not allow establishing competition in the market as it is faced in a monopoly (Visser and McIntosh 1998).

4.1.4 *Causing Economic Instability*

Considering interest as one of the causes of instabilities in the economy is another reason for the objection to it. It is claimed that it has a specific role in the emergence of economic crises (Visser and McIntosh 1998).

A sign of this apprehension is observed in Keynes' (2013) assertion. Although he is a theorist of an interest-based monetary system, Keynes indicated that the interest rate is not adjusted by the system automatically to the most efficient level for the society. Instead, it inclines to increase excessively. Therefore, an authority should keep it at an acceptable level by taking legal measures or using customs and enforcement of social norms.

Another point of view regarding the relation of interest with the stability of the economy might be Adam Smith's assertion of the need to limit the interest rate. Smith (1776) claimed that loans at high-interest rates might not be of good quality. When the interest rate is high, the wasteful people, rather than the conscious ones, borrow most of the supplied capital. Unlike the wasteful people, the alert borrowers use the loan efficiently and incline more to pay the loan back.

4.1.5 *Discounting the Future*

The relation between today and tomorrow is very important in economic decision-making. In many economic issues, today's decisions affect future behaviors and realizing the plans need to take some actions at present. In this regard, the role of interest in discounting the future is another reason asserted for objection to interest-based transactions. Since the return of compound interest from capital is attractive, people overuse natural resources to acquire capital as earliest as possible. Thus, as the discount rate that is closely relevant to the interest rate increases, the resources deplete faster. Such an attitude causes people to ignore the needs of future generations and to exploit the future for present wealth (Visser and McIntosh 1998; El Diwany 2011).

4.1.6 *High Cost on Investment and Development*

People tend to save more when the interest rate is high. Hence, investment is supported more by the interest rate via increased savings. However, it is also claimed that the high interest rate raises the cost of investment and negatively impacts the whole economy (Farooq 2012). On the other hand, the existence of interest makes the capital owners lazy and avarice due to receiving the riskless yield of loaned capital without working. When only the borrowers worry about the efficiency of the activities relevant to loans used, the overall development cannot be realized.

A similar dilemma is about the foreign debts of the undeveloped countries. Although international loans have a vital role in their development, loans with high-interest rates may put them into trouble about repayment and prompt to adverse effects.

4.1.7 *Causing Slavery*

Slavery was one of the most imposed sanctions in the case of loan defaults in Ancient times. Today, it is illegitimate almost in all countries. However, some practices similar to slavery are being observed in various regions, where people work for peanuts under bad conditions.

Regarding the issue of lending, interest legally causes a form of slavery (Erdem 2018). In modern days, the income of a borrower is one of the main sureties of the loan, and when it defaults, the lender seizes a good part of the borrower's income until the liability is met. In the modern form of slavery, unlike the slaves of Ancient times, the borrower has to take care of her daily bread herself.

4.2 The Instruments of Regulating Interest Rates

The prohibition of interest and limiting the interest rate are not only being made through legal means but also religious beliefs, social norms of ethics, and financial instruments are used. The tools that use the four sources of enforcement are reviewed in the following.

4.2.1 *Religious Beliefs*

The oldest and most prevalent regulations of interest rates were made presumably by religions. The eastern religions of Hinduism and Buddhism and the Abrahamic ones of Judaism, Christianity, and Islam, condemned, forbade, scorned interest, and restricted its practice by various approaches (Visser and McIntosh 1998).

In the last centuries BC, Hindu law forbade lending at interest for the upper classes and allowed it for Hindu temples. The Laws of Manu declared legal limits for interest rates and defined lending above the legal limit to be usurious and outlaw in the second century AD (Visser and McIntosh 1998).

Interest-based loans were not allowed in Christianity and Islam. According to the traditional and widely accepted Islamic view, interest is still considered a big sin and strictly prohibited. It was so in Judaism for lending to Jews, but loans made to others than Jews were allowed (Visser and McIntosh 1998).

In the fourth century, the Roman Catholic Church prohibited the clergy to lend at interest (Visser and McIntosh 1998). In the eleventh century, interest-based loans were decreed sin due to being a form of robbery. In the next century, forward sales at a price above the cash price were declared usurious by Pope Alexander III. Since usury was uncharitable and avarice, the usurers were excommunicated for being sinners. Saint Thomas Aquinas, in the thirteenth century, defined usury to be evil. Following the evolution in Protestant countries, in the nineteenth century, the Catholic Church allowed everyone to lend and borrow at interest. However, the interest rate could not be over the maximum level defined by the Church (Homer 1963).

Until the twelfth century, usury was condemned, and its prohibition enforced diversely in various countries and regions. Despite the lack of standard enforcement, the fear of the sin of usury was efficient on the religious and administrative leaders, merchants, and bankers (Homer 1963). The Church was organizing sermon campaigns and charging priests to travel and warn the usurers about that unless they repented and gave the interest back to the borrowers, they would go to hell. In the twelfth century, the Church instructed the clergy to excommunicate all known usurers (Graeber 2011).

4.2.2 *Social Norms*

The ethical norms of the communities are effective in enforcing the regulations of the interest rates. Lending at interest has widely been considered disrespectable in many societies.

In the fifth century BC, for example, lending at interest was considered dishonorable by the Iranians (Homer 1963). In Ancient Greece, during the lifetime of Aristotle, interest-based loans were hated and considered unnatural and honorless (Olechnowicz 2011).

The consideration of usury is similar today. According to Graeber (2011), any lender that charges interest would not be approached with sympathy all over the world. Insomuch that, the perception about the lenders might be the worst among all professionals. However, unlike the others, usurers are interestingly in the wealthiest group.

4.2.3 *Legal arrangements*

Ancient Babylonia's Code of Hammurabi is the oldest known legal arrangement that established a rule regarding interest usage, in the second century BC. The Code defined a legal upper limit for the interest rate and stated that any lender, who lends at an interest rate over the legal limit, cannot claim any repayment for the loan (Homer 1963). In some cases, the authorities of ancient Mesopotamia intervened in the interest-based transactions directly. For instance, the debts of widows and orphans were abolished several times in Sumer, Babylonia, and Assyria (Graeber 2011).

Twelve Tables of ancient Rome defined a legal upper limit for the interest rate and a penalty for the lenders that receive higher interest than the legal limit (Homer 1963). The prohibition of loans at interest in 340 BC by the Lex Genucia reforms did not take long (Visser and McIntosh 1998).

In the era of the Eastern Roman Empire, there were legal upper limits for interest rates, and accumulated interest was not allowed to exceed the principal (Homer 1963).

During the reign of Charlemagne, at the end of the eighth century, the Church's earlier prohibitions of interest were adopted as state law. However, the Jews were excluded and accepted as legal moneylenders (Geisst 2013).

Today, there are legal arrangements for the regulation of interest rates all over the world. Interest-bearing loans and activities are banned by law in some of the Muslim-populated countries. In many other countries, including the developed economies, there are legally defined ceilings on interest rates of various transactions (Glaeser and Scheinkman 1994; Reifner et al. 2010).

The interest rate ceilings are determined by either the criminal law or private laws for different types of loans. There are also arrangements defining the rate of default interest. The ceilings may be at an absolute level or a relative rate based on a reference level. Various institutions supervise the relevant regulations. The violators of the law are punished by reducing the loan, revocating the license for lending, imprisoning, and fining (Reifner et al. 2010).

4.2.4 Financial Instruments

In ancient Babylonia, the temples had great wealth and often lent to the poor people at low interest rates. These rates were well below the market rates, such as one-half or one-third of the legal limit. Even sometimes, the loans made to poor people were free of interest (Homer 1963). Since poor people were ready to borrow at higher interest rates due to desperation, the interventions of the temples should have lowered market interest rates.

The financial instruments are being widely used in the regulation of interest rates besides other means today. The cost increasing fees of insurance, broker, account holding, and maintenance have regulatory impacts on the interest rates. The arrangements on the amount, number, and period of the installments of the loan and the restrictions on its duration and total amount are influential on the interest rates (Reifner et al. 2010).

The restrictions on credit card operations are also used in the regulation of interest rates. When the debt of a credit card is not paid on the due date, some interest is charged. In general, the interest rate of delayed payment is limited. Besides, the amount of the preapproved credit of the credit card and the interest rate charged for it are also limited. Limiting the interest rate of a defaulted debt and the amount and interest rate of credit has impacts on the market's interest rates (DeMuth 1986).

Another example is the influence of the reserve requirement ratios of the central banks on the market interest rate. The reserve requirement ratios are among the determinants of the cost of bank credits. The interest rates in the market are controlled through the credit costs imposed by the use of the reserve requirement ratios (Montoro and Moreno 2011).

The instruments practiced in regulating interest rates are exemplified in four groups of enforcement sources in Table 4.1.

Table 4.1 Some examples of the instruments used in interest rate control

Source of enforcement	*Examples of instruments*
Religious beliefs	– Both the Eastern and Abrahamic religions condemned, forbade, and scorned interest – Hindu law defined lending above the legal limit to be usurious – Judaism and Christianity did not allow interest-based lending – The usurers were excommunicated for being uncharitable and avarice, and deserving of hell – Interest is still considered a sin and strictly prohibited in Islam
Social norms of ethics	– Interest was considered dishonorable by the Iranians Interest-based loans were hated and considered unnatural and honorless in ancient Greece – Lending at interest was disrespectable in many ancient societies. It is the same in many modern communities
Legal arrangements	– Code of Hammurabi and Twelve Tables defined legal upper interest rate limits – The authorities of ancient Mesopotamia abolished the interest-based debts of widows and orphans several times – In the Eastern Roman Empire, the accumulated interest was not allowed to exceed the principal – Interest is banned by law in some Muslim-populated countries – Many economies, including the developed ones, have legally defined ceilings on the interest rates
Financial instruments	– The temples lent to the poor people at quite low-interest rates in ancient Babylonia, which should have lowered market rates – The cost increasing fees of insurance, broker, account holding, and maintenance have regulatory impacts on the interest rates – The arrangements on the amount, number, and period of the installments of the loan and the restrictions on its duration and total amount have impacts on the interest rates – The reserve requirement ratios of the central banks affect the market rate of interest by changing the cost of bank credits

References

Böhm-Bawerk, Eugen. 1890. *Capital and Interest: A Critical History of Economical Theory*. London: Macmillan.

Caskey, John P. 1994. *Fringe Banking: Check-Cashing Outlets, Pawnshops, and the Poor*. Russell Sage Foundation.

Choudhury, Masudul Alam, and Uzir Abdul Malik. 1992. *The Foundations of Islamic Political Economy*. London: Palgrave Macmillan. https://public.ebookcentral.proquest.com/choice/publicfullrecord.aspx?p=5652786.

Chown, John F. 1996. *A History of Money: From AD 800*. London: Routledge.

Coco, Giuseppe, and David De Meza. 2009. In Defense of Usury Laws. *Journal of Money, Credit and Banking* 41 (8): 1691–1703.

DeLorenzo, Yusuf Talal. 2006. "Introduction to Understanding Riba." In *Interest in Islamic Economics: Understanding Riba*, edited by Abdulkadir Thomas, 1–9. New York: Routledge.

DeMuth, Christopher C. 1986. "The Case against Credit Card Interest Rate Regulation." *Yale Journal on Regulation* 3 (2): 201–242.

Durkin, Thomas A. 1993. "An Economic Perspective on Interest Rate Limitations." *Georgia State University Law Review* 9 (4).

El Diwany, Tarek. 2011. *Faiz Sorunu [The Problem with Interest]*. İstanbul: İz Yayıncılık.

Erdem, Ekrem. 2018. "Kur'an'da Riba (Faiz) Ayetlerinin Kademeli Nüzulü ve Üslubu: İslam'ın Ticaret, Infak ve Finans Sistemi Üzerinden Bir Inceleme [The Gradual Revelation and Style of the Riba (Interest) Verses in Quran: An Enquiry Regarding the Trade, Aid and Finance System of Islam]." In *İslam Iktisadı Perspektifinden Faiz [Interest from the Perspective of Islamic Economics]*, edited by Taha Eğri and Zeynep Hafsa Orhan, 1–51. İstanbul: İktisat Yayınları.

Farooq, Muhammad. 2012. "Interest, Usury and Its Impact on the Economy." *Dialogue* 7 (3): 265–76.

Geisst, Charles R. 2013. *Beggar Thy Neighbor: A History of Usury and Debt*. Philadelphia: University of Pennsylvania Press.

Glaeser, Edward L., and Jose A. Scheinkman. 1994. "Neither a Borrower Nor a Lender Be: An Economic Analysis of Interest Restrictions and Usury Laws." 4954. National Bureau of Economic Research.

Graeber, David. 2011. *Debt: The First 5000 Years*. New York: Melville House Publishing.

Homer, Sidney. 1963. *A History of Interest Rates*. Hoboken, NJ: Rutgers University Press.

Kennedy, Margrit. 1995. *Interest and Inflation Free Money*. Seva International.

Keynes, John Maynard. 2013. *The Collected Writings of John Maynard Keynes-The General Theory of Employment, Interest and Money*, vol. VII. New York: Cambridge University Press.

Khan, Muhammad Akram. 2013. *What Is Wrong with Islamic Economics? Analysing the Present State and Future Agenda*. Cheltenham, UK: Edward Elgar.

Lewison, Martin. 1999. "Conflicts of Interest? The Ethics of Usury." *Journal of Business Ethics* 22 (4): 327–39.

Montoro, Carlos, and Ramon Moreno. 2011. "The Use of Reserve Requirements as a Policy Instrument in Latin America." *BIS Quarterly Review, March* March: 53–65.

Olechnowicz, Cheryl A. 2011. "History of Usury: The Transition of Usury through Ancient Greece, the Rise of Christianity and Islam, and the Expansion of Long-Distance Trade and Capitalism." *Gettysburg Economic Review* 5: 97–109.

Reifner, Udo, Sebastien Clerc-Renaud, and R.A. Michael Knobloch. 2010. "Study on Interest Rate Restrictions in the EU." ETD/2009/IM/H3/87. Institut für Finanzdienstleistungen.

Rougeau, Vincent D. 1996. "Rediscovering Usury: An Argument for Legal Controls on Credit Card Interest Rates." *University of Colorado Law Review* 67 (1): 1–46.

Shahar, Wan Shahzlinda Shah Wan, Ummi Munirah Syuhada Mohamad Zan, and Wan Suraya Wan Hassin. 2016. "The Implication of Usury (Riba) in Economic: A Critique." In *Proceeding of the 3rd International Conference on Management & Muamalah 2016*.

Sharawy, Hesham M. 2000. "Understanding the Islamic Prohibition of Interest: A Guide to Aid Economic Cooperation Between the Islamic and Western Worlds." *Georgia Journal of International and Comparative Law* 29 (1): 153–179.

Smith, Adam. 1776. *The Wealth of Nations*. The Electric Book Co.

Visser, Wayne A.M., and Alastair McIntosh. 1998. "A Short Review of the Historical Critique of Usury." *Accounting, Business & Financial History* 8 (2): 175–189.

CHAPTER 5

Interest Rate Control

Although there are scholars, including some eminent pro-interest ones (Smith 1776; Keynes 2013), defending regulation of interest (Metwally 1990; Glaeser and Scheinkman 1994; Rougeau 1996; Coco and De Meza 2009; Lee 2017; Cheng 2018), today, most of the economists do not support any ceiling on the interest rate (Durkin 1993). The opponents of interest rate regulations justify their stance by warning about various undesired consequences of interest rate control that have distortive effects on the market and the whole economy. However, in practice, interest is still being widely regulated directly or implicitly all over the world.

Interest is considered as the price of loaned capital, and its regulation is a sort of price control. Hence, the concept of *price control* is introduced in the first section of this chapter. The mechanism of price control and its various consequences are evaluated. Steven Cheung's (1974) price control model, which is possible to apply to any price control regulation, is also presented in the first section to evaluate the probable effects of interest rate control on the market. In the second section, the implications of interest rate regulations on various markets, the individuals, and the whole economy are reviewed.

C. Eyerci, *The Causes and Consequences of Interest Theory*, https://doi.org/10.1007/978-3-030-78702-8_5

5.1 The Price Control and Cheung's Model

The limitation imposed by an authority on the price of a good or service is named *price control*. The restriction may be a price ceiling that does not allow prices above the maximum as in rent control or a price floor that does not allow prices below the minimum as in the wage floor (Coyne and Coyne 2015a). The subject of control is not always the wages and the prices of goods and services. There are some other control areas, such as rent control and agricultural subsidies. As being the price of loaned capital, interest is also a subject of price control. The limitations on the interest rates are among the sorts of price ceilings.

Price controls, including wage controls, are being implemented to.

- Tackle inflation (Lipsey 1977; Schuettinger and Butler 1979; Miller 2015),
- Overcome shortages (Schuettinger and Butler 1979),
- Protect the consumers from black-market and exploitation (Karadaği 2018),
- Prevent monopoly (Tabakoğlu 2016),
- Achieve equity in the workplace (Siebert 2015),
- Prevent profiteering by property owners (Bourne 2015),
- Prevent price wars,
- Ensure fair returns to the factors of production,
- Eliminate the cost of information,
- Stabilize the market during an emergency,
- Ensure equitable distribution of benefits and costs of exchange (Bashar 1997).

Price controls have always been used prevalently since ancient times. Fixed levels were decreed for each price in ancient Egypt. Contrary to modern times, the established wage ceilings were only aiming to keep the workers alive. The wages and prices were controlled by the authorities also in ancient Mesopotamia. Specifically, in Babylonia, earnings of many types of workers, prices of various goods, and rents were explicitly determined by the Code of Hammurabi (Schuettinger and Butler 1979).

In ancient China, the Confucian doctrine asserted that the intervention of authority in the economy was required to keep the competition at a minimum. Accordingly, the government regulated many issues of economic life, including the prices, and determined the mechanism of the supervision of the regulations (Huan-Chang 1911).

In ancient Athens, shortages were frequent, and the increased prices due to shortages were not allowed to exceed the limits set by the government. The prices of some products were fixed to a proportion of the prices of the raw materials. For example, the ratio of the price of bread to the price of barley or wheat was determined (Schuettinger and Butler 1979).

In various periods of the long life of the Roman Republic and Empire, the prices and wages were controlled by ceilings and floors. In the following times, in medieval Europe, the concept of *just price* emerged as a religious belief. Excessive profiting from trade and stockpiling were condemned. The authorities controlled the prices of the goods and the wages. In England, for example, after the Black Death in 1348, half of the population died, a shortage of workers emerged, and the payments multiplied. The government limited the wages by law, but many workers refused to work at lowered wages (Schuettinger and Butler 1979).

Price controls were also implemented in the Muslim world, specifically in the Ottoman Empire. Although the original approach of Islamic thought refused any control and left the formation of price to the market, the rejection of price control was reevaluated afterward and redefined to be valid, at least in the perfect competition markets. For the imperfect markets, specifically in the case of monopolies, price control is considered the sole remedy (Bashar 1997; Tabakoğlu 2016). For example, although he was supporting an economic system based on the free market, a prominent medieval Muslim scholar Ibn Taimiyah did not oppose imposing price control in some situations such as imperfect markets and disasters. Even so, he warned against excessive interventions in order not to undermine the people's profit motive (Ghazanfar and Islahi 2003).

In the early times of the American Colonies and France after the Revolution, the controls were in use. During the two World Wars, the price and wage controls were active almost in all warring countries (Schuettinger and Butler 1979). The United States Government established the Office of Price Administration as a regulatory body during the Second World War, for a primary task of price control. Afterward, some other missions were carried out by the office, such as rationing. Rationing was considered critical in the success of price control (Galbraith 1946; Bronfenbrenner 1947). Wage and price control policies were being carried out by the United States and United Kingdom governments still in the 1970s (Coyne and Coyne 2015a).

5.1.1 The Mechanism and Consequences of Price Control

Price controls were used in the past and are still being used today. The controls aim to solve the problems in the market or prevent the emergence of new ones. However, it is also widely realized that the interventions have undesired consequences, some of which have distortive effects on the market. Even in some cases, the controls cause permanent damages (Schuettinger and Butler 1979) to the market.

Interestingly, some controls were claimed to cause results just opposite to the intention. The efforts to tackle inflation are given as such an example. Fixing or limiting the prices of goods has been a measure often taken to fight inflation. Although these controls decrease inflation for a short time, they have adverse effects on the long-run (Miller 2015; Schuettinger and Butler 1979). Long-continued control policies cause price stickiness, and consequently, the price ceilings tend to become price floors (Booth and Davies 2015).

Masking of the real reasons for the economic troubles is another undesired implication of price control. Repressing inflation by price control, for example, might be a result of neglecting the role of monetary policy in the fight against inflation. Similarly, a minimum wage policy may prevent the observation of the effects of low productivity that emerged due to an inappropriate education system (Coyne and Coyne , 2015b).

The distinction between the short-run and the long-run, regarding the effects of price control in fighting inflation, is generalized, including all other types of controls, by some scholars. It is asserted that the short-run benefits of the restrictions are small and transitory, but the long-run costs are high and persistent (Lipsey 1977).

Even so, there are scholars either supporting or opposing price controls. Besides, a third group makes a distinction between the temporariness and continuity of the restrictions while evaluating price controls. The needs for and benefits from regulations may not be the same in a perfectly competitive market and an imperfect market (Bronfenbrenner 1947; Vandenbrink 1982; DeMuth 1986; Tabakoğlu 2016). In case of the existence of a monopsony in a labor market, a price floor for wages may be essential. In the case of a disaster such as a hurricane or an earthquake, price ceilings may help to prevent excessive prices (Schmidtz 2016).

In some cases, price controls may help to postpone the problems, and thus, they may help to find time for the preparation of efficient solutions. It may be possible to reduce the inflationary expectations for a short time that is effective in fighting inflation. A delay in price movement may also be useful to make structural changes in the economy (Lipsey 1977).

In sum, the price ceiling and price floor are the two types of price controls that have similar mechanisms working in opposite directions.

5.1.1.1 Price Ceiling

The supply–demand curve in case of price control as a price ceiling is illustrated in Fig. 5.1. The market-clearing price is P_M with an exchange amount of Q_M when there is not any price control. A price ceiling over the market price does not affect the market. With a price ceiling as it is showed by P_C in the figure, the exchange cannot be made at a price over the ceiling, and the exchanged quantity (Q_S) is defined by the supply side. Q_S is below the exchanged quantity (Q_M) at the market-clearing price. On the other hand, since the ceiling price (P_C) is lower than the

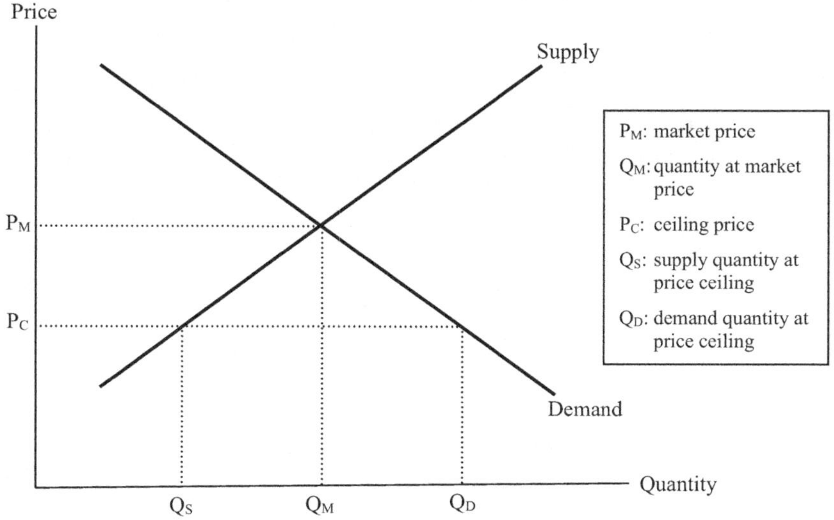

Fig. 5.1 The supply–demand curve with price ceiling

market-clearing price (P_M), the quantity of demand (Q_D) is higher than Q_M. Thus, a shortage will emerge due to the difference between the quantities of demand and supply at the ceiling price (Q_D–Q_S).

Although some demanders are willing to pay more than the ceiling price, the control regulation does not allow it, and the shortage continues. The price ceiling reduces the number of exchange transactions causing a consequent decrease in the quantity of supply. Thus, the total welfare decreases.

The price ceilings reduce the incentive to invest in the commodities that have controlled prices. For the same reason, the existing producers do not have any incentive to improve the quality of the goods they produce. Moreover, the effects of price control may not be observed in the short-run, and when they appear, the reason for their adverse effects may not be correctly determined due to the time passed. Thus, the problem will not be solved (Coyne and Coyne 2015b).

On the other hand, because the demand is higher than the supply, there are difficulties in the determination of the demanders, which will receive the scarce loan. Such challenges increase transaction costs.

Price control on the ticket of a show, for example, causes queues in front of the tollbooths, at which the first come first served. The ones, who are late or do not want to wait, may seek alternative solutions. They may bribe to the officers to have the ticket, or they may buy it from the black market at a higher rate.

When price regulation does not allow to rent an estate over the ceiling, the number of rentals decreases and a shortage emerges. If the control is on the low-rated estates, the owners may enhance the quality of their properties and exclude them from the scope of the regulation (McKenzie and Lee 2010). If all rate levels are controlled, the owners will decrease the expenditure for the maintenance of the estate, then, the quality of the existing properties gets worse. In the long-run, the construction of new estates will reduce (Lipsey 1977). The destructive effect of rent control may be high to the extent that the regulation is described as the most efficient known way to destroy a city except bombing (Bourne 2015).

The price control on fares of services provided through fixed infrastructures has some other implications. A price ceiling imposed on rail fares, for example, causes an increment in demand. The effect of the increased demand is similar to the shortage that emerged in the abovementioned cases. Some routes of trains become overcrowded at some hours by the increased number of passengers. That is a cost for both passengers and operators. Whereas, being able to arrange the fares concerning the routes and hours could help to use the existing capacity in a better way (Wellings 2015).

Some cases of price ceilings and probable consequences of the regulations are summarized in Table 5.1.

Table 5.1 Some cases of price ceilings and probable consequences

The price arrangement	*Probable outcomes*
Limited price of a show	– Queues in front of the tollbooths – Bribes given to the officers by the latecomers – Emergence of a black market
Limited rates of rentals	– Decrease in the number of rentals – Decrease in the expenditure for the maintenance of the estates and worsening in the quality of the existing properties – Reduction in the construction of new estates
Limited prices of rail fares	– Overcrowding of some routes at some hours by the increased number of passengers due to increased demand – Increase in the cost for both the passengers and operators
Limited prices of consumer goods	– Decrease in the quality of the goods – Shortage due to the decreased incentive for the production of the goods – Decrease in inflation for a short time – Emergence of price stickiness and the tendency of price ceiling to became price floor on the long-run

5.1.1.2 Price Floor

The supply–demand curve in the case of price control in the form of a price floor is illustrated in Fig. 5.2. P_M is again the market-clearing price, and Q_M is the exchanged quantity without any price control. This time, there is no need to think on a price floor that is lower than or equal to the market price. P_F, the price floor is the minimum level of price at which exchanges can be made. Thus, the exchanged quantity (Q_D) is defined by the demand side. Q_D is below the exchanged quantity (Q_M) at the market-clearing price. Again, this time, since the floor price (PF) is higher than the market-clearing price (P_M), the quantity of supply (Q_S)

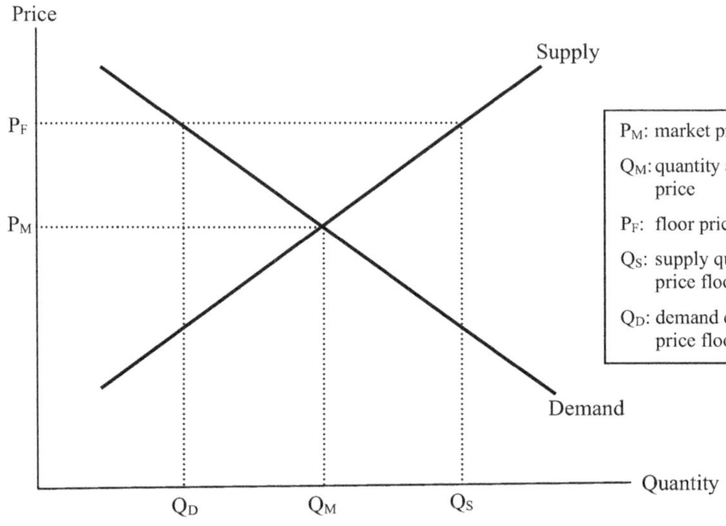

Fig. 5.2 The supply–demand curve with price floor

is higher than Q_M. The difference between the quantities of the supply and demand at floor price (Q_s–Q_D) is the excess supply.

In the case of a minimum wage as a price floor, the demand for labor decreases by the implementation of control regulation, but, on the contrary, a new group of candidates, who would not be willing to work for the market wage before the control, will emerge, and the supply of labor will increase. Then, in a labor market of excess supply, some workers, who are contented to work at lower wages, will have to compete with others that would not be their rivals at lower market wages. Presumably, in such a case, the less qualified workers will not be able to find a job, or if they are employed, they will have the risk of losing their jobs (Siebert 2015). While expecting the wage control to prevent the workers, specifically the less qualified ones, from the exploitation of the employers, it may have an adverse effect causing some workers to be unemployed.

Regarding the fortunate employed ones, the wage paid by the employer to some overqualified workers will be higher than the payment that would be made to the sufficiently qualified workers if it could be possible. Although equity in the workplace is aimed by the wage floor (Siebert 2015), the workers that have various qualifications will receive the same wage, what it conversely means inequity. On the other hand, the overqualified workers will not be satisfied with their jobs, their productivity will decrease, and a high turnover rate of the workers will be observed, implying many further problems.

Besides, the minimum wage enforcement increases the cost of labor, specifically in the unskilled-worker intensive sectors. The increased cost may cause to employ fewer workers or may make the employer stop activity. Either of these will reduce the employment further.

The price floors are also being used by defining minimum price levels for some goods to make their availability costly. For example, to prevent excessive drinking, price floors are imposed on alcoholic drinks. However, it is claimed that the benefit of the minimum unit price for alcoholic beverages is not much as expected, for the high-income heavy drinkers. Conversely, the cost of the control for the remaining drinkers is more than estimated. On the supply side, the regulation of minimum pricing may lead the producers to sell expensive products more and to spend more on marketing (Snowdon 2015).

Implementation of price floors in two cases and the probable outcomes of the price control policies are listed in Table 5.2.

5.1.1.3 Signaling Role of Price

In addition to many case-specific implications, price control also has some common consequences due to the price's implicit role in the market. Any efficient decision made in the market requires too much and detailed information. To decide on production, for example, one must answer many questions such as which product is demanded by the consumers; what quality does make a product marketable; at what cost will production be profitable; how much must be paid to labor; which raw material is worth to use? All the individuals in a market have too many questions that are possible to answer with too much information.

However, although it is not possible to have all the information needed for each individual, everyone makes her own decision of production and consumption, in other words, what to sell and buy. The mentioned coordination is not made centrally by an authority, but it emerges spontaneously by the signaling role of the price (Schmidtz 2016). Price does not tell anything explicitly about the needed information, but it transmits a composite signal that comprises all the relevant information. Thus, it is considered crucial for being a fast and efficient transmitter of information (Sowell 1980) that is crucial in the coordination of market activities.

Table 5.2 Some cases of price floors and probable consequences

The price arrangement	*Probable outcomes*
Minimum wage	– Decrease in demand for labor – Increase in the supply of labor due to a new group of candidates, who would not be willing to work for the market wage before the control – Difficulties of some workers, who are contented to work at lower wages, in competing with others that would not be their rivals at market wages – The less qualified workers' increased risk of losing their jobs due to the new candidates by the wage control policy – Increase in the cost of labor, specifically in the unskilled-worker intensive sectors – Employment of fewer workers or termination of the activity due to the increased labor cost
Minimum unit price for an alcoholic beverage	– Increase in the cost of its availability as desired – Less benefit than expected for the high-income heavy drinkers – More costly than estimated for the remaining drinkers – Increase in the sales of expensive products – Increase in marketing expenditure

There is continuous and rapid development in the structure of the relations within the economy, and price makes it possible to follow the change (Lavoie 1985).

Under a price control policy, transmitting and receiving signals about the changes that affect the prices in the economy is usually defective. The lack of signaling prevents to appropriately use the resources for real economic developments and cause a loss in welfare (Coyne and Coyne 2015b).

5.1.2 Cheung's Price Control Model

Steven N.S. Cheung's (1974) price control model applies to any price control regulation, including the interest rate regulations. The model is appropriate for the evaluation of the probable effects of interest rate regulation on the market.

Cheung stated that the correct evaluation of the results of a price control regulation requires the specification of constraints proper to the real market practice. However, any effective control is complicated, and it is hard to estimate them correctly. To specify the constraints, it is needed to analyze the real-world situation. On the other hand, such an analysis can be made within a theoretical framework, which helps to determine the relevant and significant constraints. Even so, since the effectiveness of price controls varies by time and place, the associated constraints are still many to be considered in the evaluation of the influences of price control. Simplification would help, but the more simplification causes the less appearance of the implications.

Therefore, as a solution to the abovementioned problem, Cheung (1974) developed a price control theory, asserting some proposals about the investigation method of constraints relevant to any price intervention rather than explaining the implications of a specific control operation. The propositions are accordant with economic principles.

Since the price controls are restrictions on the income that originates from private contracts, the asserted propositions are strictly relevant to property rights and agreements. To define as private property, the owner of an asset has to have three privileges. At first, the owner should have the right to use, decide how to use, and prevent others from the use of the asset. Second, the owner should have the right to receive income from the use of the asset by others. Thirdly, the owner should have the right to transfer the ownership of the asset to any other individual by selling or granting.

A restriction on the exercise of any of these three privileges, which decreases the income received, has adverse implications on the others. Since a person tries to maximize the utility from the private property, the property may be used by the owner himself if the usage is considered the most valuable choice, or the usage or the ownership may be transferred to another person by a contractual agreement. Either a restriction on the most valuable use of a property or a constraint on the transferability of its usage or ownership decreases the value of the property. Basing on the presented framework, Cheung (1974) developed two propositions.

According to his first proposition, while controlling a price, if a party's revenue is taken away and the right of diverted income is not exclusively assigned to someone else, it tends to dissipate. It may occur in three ways. First, the form of the usage or production of the good may change, and this may cause a decrease in the good's value. Secondly, contractual behavior may change by causing an increase in the cost of drawing up or enforcing contracts. Finally, the two may occur together.

An example may be helpful to observe the mechanism of the emergence of nonexclusive income due to price control. When the monthly market rent of $100 of an estate is reduced to $60 by law, the reduced $40 that was received by the owner of the estate before is generally not become an exclusive income of a specific party. The renter may not receive some part or the whole of $40.

Exclusively assigning a part of the useable area of the estate that is corresponding to $40 rent to the renter would prevent the dissipation. The owner's remaining portion will receive a $60 income appropriate to the defined limit. Another solution may be exclusively transferring the rights on the part of the rent taken from the owner to the renter. By the implementation of either solution, some additional costs will emerge, and the proprietor and the renter will be joint owners of the estate. Thus, the estate would be used as if there was no control. If the law, however, prevents the renter from being a joint owner, the rights on a portion of the estate cannot exclusively be assigned to the renter.

A well-prepared legal arrangement may help the renter in exclusively claiming for the portion of the rent. However, when the law is not complete enough, the competition of the contracting parties will cause the nonexclusive income to dissipate.

The second proposition claims that, in case of the existence of nonexclusive income tending to dissipate, the parties try to minimize the dissipation. Thus, they seek an alternative way of usage or production of a good to lower the decrease in its value or draw up alternative contractual arrangements to lessen the increase in the transaction costs. Taking a combined action is the third way.

The contracting parties regard the dissipated income due to not being exclusively assigned to an individual as waste, and try to minimize it. Observing and specifying the constraints that help with the minimization of dissipation would be essential for this purpose. Thus, the implications of price control may be explained.

In a case as in the abovementioned example, to assign the \$40 rent to the renter exclusively without making him a joint owner of the estate, enforcement of a complete legal arrangement is needed. Such a regulation must state that the owner of the estate can never dispossess the renter, define the obligations of the parties about the maintenance and repair of the estate, assign exclusive use rights to the renter, and grant the right to sublet the estate partly or wholly to the renter. Lack of any item will prevent to assign income to the renter exclusively.

Although the owners who already rented their estates when complete and detailed legislation of control takes effect have to obey the regulation, the owners of not rented estates have the opportunity to exclude the renters who claim to contract under the controlled conditions. The latter group may prefer to use the estates themselves, sell the estates, or rent them to others that are considered more appropriate. However, any alternative decision will bring more transaction costs compared to the case before the legislation took effect, in which there was a monthly rental income of \$100.

The owner of such an estate weighs the value of using the estate himself less than \$100 in general. On the other hand, he can make an alternative contractual arrangement at a higher transaction cost. There will be income dissipation in both cases.

If the owner weighs the value of using the estate himself less than \$60, he would prefer to rent it to the first claimant renter at a monthly rate of \$60. Then, the candidate renters will compete to be the primary applicant by spending time and effort. However, since the owner has the right to exclude some candidates and to choose whomever he wants as the renter, the candidates will try to offer the least costly arrangement that maintains the least dissipation for the income of the owner. If the law allows, a solution to the problem may be the competition of the candidate renters in buying the estate instead of renting. If this is not permitted or its arrangement costs much, the candidates may compete in paying key money to the owner that will be a rate less than \$40. If the second option is also not allowed somehow, the furniture used in the estate may be rented or sold to the renter at an overvalued rate. Each alternative has distinct transaction costs. As the alternative arrangement is restricted more by the supervision and enforcement provisions of the law, the transaction costs of the regulation will be higher.

After evaluating the responses of the parties of various transactions that are exposed to price control, Cheung (1974) asserted that price control redistributes the wealth as any other regulation of market transactions. Then, he sought a way of management of private contracts not to affect the resource allocation and proposed to meet two conditions in line with Coase's (1960) theory. Firstly, the redistributed income rights among the parties should be assigned clearly and exclusively to them. Secondly, making alternative contracts and the enforcement of the regulations should not emerge extra costs.

5.2 The Consequences of Interest Rate Control

Interest rate control is probably the oldest form of price control, as it was amply exemplified in the relevant chapters. Since a definition of the interest rate is the price of the use of a loan, interest rate control has some effects on the market, similar to the market distortive consequences of other price controls. Due to having many undesired results, most of the economists object to interest rate ceilings.

A price ceiling on the interest rate that is not allowed to be exceeded reduces the supply of loans and increases the demand for it. Just like any other price control policy, such intervention causes a shortage. Besides the decrease in the total supply of loans, the control also reduces the diversity of the products (Booth and Davies 2015). The decreased supply of loans cannot meet the increased demand for the loan, and the borrowers may not be able to find wholly appropriate loan products.

In markets of mortgage, for example, where interest rate ceilings were below the market rates, it was observed that the quantity of the loans was less, and the term of credit was shorter than the ones in not controlled markets. The effect of the rate ceiling on the credit volume and duration was similar in nonmortgage credit markets (DeMuth 1986).

The shortage of loans has some different effects from the shortages of other goods or services that lead to queues, bribes, black markets, etc. In case of a loan shortage, the lender discriminates the risky borrowers from others, and the more needy ones lose the opportunity to borrow. The cheap loan attracts some less needy borrowers, who would not borrow at a higher interest rate, and the needier and risky borrowers, who are ready and able to borrow at a higher interest rate, cannot find any loan at the controlled level (Durkin 1993; Ellison and Forster 2008; Rigbi 2013).

The less needy borrowers, who find the opportunity of the relatively cheap loan, may not act rationally and not use the capital efficiently. Although one of the aims of interest rate control is preventing or at least reducing the profiteering of people, the borrowers may tend to be profiteers by the perception of gravy.

The shortage of loans may guide the desperate borrowers excluded from the ordinary loan market to usurers, pawnshops, or loan sharks (Rigbi 2013; Booth and Davies 2015). These may be legal but are mostly illegal, unlicensed (Ellison and Forster 2008) lenders similar to the black markets of other controlled goods.

On the other hand, the cost of the loan for the low-income needy borrowers that find the chance to borrow at a controlled rate may be higher than as it was in a freely operating market (Ellison and Forster 2008). In the credit card market, for example, there may be a ceiling imposed on the interest rate of the credit used by a credit card below the market interest rate without controlling the lump-sum fees. In such a case, the lenders attempt to cover the loss for the controlled rate by increasing the yearly lump-sum card fee (DeMuth 1986). Compared to the unregulated case, the new cost may be more harmful to the financially weak card users.

The interest rate ceilings are also expected to protect low-income borrowers from over-indebtedness. Unfortunately, it is observed that the rate control may increase the debts of low-income borrowers and may lead them to manage the loan by rolling over the debt (Ellison and Forster 2008). Paradoxically, although the interest rate control is aiming to protect the low-income consumers and financially weak, small businesses with a motivation of justice, the consequences of the control policy may be far from fairness (Schmidtz 2016).

The signaling role of price in conveying information (Sowell 1980) promotes entering the market. The new agents are the most innovative and effective in the transformation of the market (Booth and Davies 2015). Thus, the new agents enhance the competition (Durkin 1993). However, any control of interest rate prevents the transmission of information. The lack of information discourages the new lenders from entering the loan market and distorts the competition in the market.

Since price control enhances the concentration of the market and harms its competitiveness (Lipsey 1977), a more competitive loan market requires deregulated interest rates or, at least, not too low-interest-rate ceilings (Vandenbrink 1982).

Not being able to receive the relevant information, the investors in the capital market are challenged by significant problems in investing. The funds may be received by the borrowers that should not survive under conditions in which the interest rate is not controlled, but not by the proper ones (Schuettinger and Butler 1979).

As Cheung (1974) proposed, a ceiling on interest rate below the market rate causes the income from the loan to dissipate. The dissipation may be the result of using the capital for a purpose rather than lending or a change in contractual behavior in a loan transaction.

The lenders' preference for using the capital for less effective plans, consuming it, for example, causes the value of the capital to decrease. A shortage of loan emerges due to the capital owners' unwillingness in lending. By the loss of the attraction of capital ownership, the potential lenders stop to save. The decreased savings keep the investment low. The low level of investment compared to the case that interest rate is free causes a decline in wealth via affecting output, employment, and income negatively (Durkin 1993).

In the case of interest rate control, the dissipation of rent due to the change in contractual behavior is about the emerged extra costs. The control regulations motivate the parties in the market to find ways to overcome the constraints. However, new costs are emerging, such as bribes, operating fees, and additional banking charges by the actions taken to overcome the limitations (Chen et al. 2015). Both additional costs of parties of an exchange and enforcement costs of the regulations are wasting the resources (Durkin 1993).

The probable consequences of interest rate control are summarized in groups of its impact channels in Table 5.3.

Table 5.3 Consequences of interest rate control

The impact channel	*Probable outcomes*
Impacts on borrowers	– Demand for loans increases – Borrowers cannot find appropriate loan products – Term of loans becomes shorter – More needy borrowers are discriminated due to being riskier – Cheap loan attracts less needy borrowers, who would not borrow at a higher interest rate – Cost of controlled rate may be higher than the cost of the free market rate, e.g., increased lump-sum fees of credit cards – Controlled rate may increase the debts of low-income borrowers by rolling over the debt – Desperate borrowers are guided to usurers, pawnshops, and loan sharks
Impacts on lenders	– Supply of loans decreases – Diversity of the loan products decreases – Capital is used for less effective purposes rather than lending – Potential lenders stop to save – The lack of information due to rate control discourages the new lenders from entering the loan market
Combined impacts on the market	– The less needy borrowers may not act rationally and not use the capital efficiently – Interest rate control prevents the transmission of information – The absence of new lenders entering the loan market distorts the competition in the market – The funds may be received by the firms that should not survive under uncontrolled market conditions – Investment decreases due to decreased savings – Decreased level of the investment adversely affects the output, employment, and income, and wealth declines – New costs such as bribes, operating fees, and additional banking charges emerge due to searching for ways to overcome the constraints

References

Bashar, Muhammad Lawal Ahmad. 1997. "Price Control in an Islamic Economy." *Journal of King Abdulaziz University: Islamic Economics* 9: 29–52.

Booth, Philip, and Stephen Davies. 2015. "Price Ceilings in Financial Markets." In *Flaws and Ceilings: Price Controls and the Damage They Cause*, edited by Christopher Coyne and Rachel Coyne, 135–57. London: Institute of Economic Affairs.

Bourne, Ryan. 2015. "The Flaws in Rent Ceilings." In *Flaws and Ceilings: Price Controls and the Damage They Cause*, edited by Christopher Coyne and Rachel Coyne, 72–95. London: Institute of Economic Affairs.

Bronfenbrenner, Martin. 1947. "Price Control Under Imperfect Competition." *The American Economic Review* 37 (1): 107–20.

Chen, Donghua, Dequan Jiang, and Xin Yu. 2015. "Corporate Philanthropy and Bank Loans in China." *Pacific-Basin Finance Journal* 35: 402–24.

Cheng, Hao. 2018. "The Death and Revival of Usury in China: An Institutional Analysis." *Journal of Economic Issues* 52 (2): 527–33.

Cheung, Steven NS. 1974. "A Theory of Price Control." *The Journal of Law and Economics* 17 (1): 53–71.

Coase, Ronald H. 1960. "The Problem of Social Cost." *The Journal of Law and Economics* 3: 1–44.

Coco, Giuseppe, and David De Meza. 2009. "In Defense of Usury Laws." *Journal of Money, Credit and Banking* 41 (8): 1691–1703.

Coyne, Christopher, and Rachel Coyne. 2015a. "Introduction." In *Flaws and Ceilings: Price Controls and the Damage They Cause*, edited by Christopher Coyne and Rachel Coyne, 1–7. London: Institute of Economic Affairs.

———. 2015b. "The Economics of Price Controls." In *Flaws and Ceilings: Price Controls and the Damage They Cause*, edited by Christopher Coyne and Rachel Coyne, 8–28. London: Institute of Economic Affairs.

DeMuth, Christopher C. 1986. "The Case Against Credit Card Interest Rate Regulation." *Yale Journal on Regulation* 3 (2): 201–42.

Durkin, Thomas A. 1993. "An Economic Perspective on Interest Rate Limitations." *Georgia State University Law Review* 9 (4).

Ellison, Anna, and Robert Forster. 2008. "The Impact of Interest Rate Ceilings: The Evidence from International Experience and the Implications for Regulation and Consumer Protection in the Credit Market in Australia." Policis. http://www.policis.com/pdf/Old/Australia_The_impact_of_interest_rate_ceilings_20080326.pdf.

Galbraith, John Kenneth. 1946. "Reflections on Price Control." *The Quarterly Journal of Economics* 60 (4): 475–89.

Ghazanfar, Shaikh M., and Abdul Azim Islahi. 2003. "Explorations in Medieval Arab-Islamic Economic Thought—Some Aspects of Ibn Taimiyah's

Economics." In *Medieval Islamic Economic Thought—Filling the Great Gap in European Economics*, edited by Shaikh M. Ghazanfar, 53–71. Rouledge-Curzon.

Glaeser, Edward L., and Jose A. Scheinkman. 1994. "Neither a Borrower Nor a Lender Be: An Economic Analysis of Interest Restrictions and Usury Laws." 4954. National Bureau of Economic Research.

Huan-Chang, Chen. 1911. *The Economic Principles of Confucius and His School*. New York: Columbia University.

Karadaği, Ali Muhyiddin. 2018. *İslam Iktisadına Giriş [An Introduction to Islamic Economics]*. İstanbul: İktisat Yayınları.

Keynes, John Maynard. 2013. *The Collected Writings of John Maynard Keynes—The General Theory of Employment, Interest and Money*. Vol. VII. New York: Cambridge University Press.

Lavoie, Don. 1985. *National Economic Planning: What Is Left?* Cambridge: Ballinger Publishing.

Lee, Joanne. 2017. "Should Interest Rates Be Regulated or Abolished? The Case for the Abolition of Usury." *The Western Australian Jurist* 8: 227–62.

Lipsey, Richard G. 1977. "Wage-Price Controls: How to Do a Lot of Harm by Trying to Do a Little Good." *Canadian Public Policy* 3 (1): 1–13.

McKenzie, Richard B., and Dwight R. Lee. 2010. *Microeconomics for MBAs: The Economic Way of Thinking for Managers*. Cambridge University Press.

Metwally, Mukhtar M. 1990. "Towards Abolishing the Rate of Interest in Contemporary Islamic Societies." *Journal of King Abdulaziz University: Islamic Economics* 2 (1): 3–23.

Miller, Robert C.B. 2015. "Price Ceilings: Ancient and Modern." In *Flaws and Ceilings: Price Controls and the Damage They Cause*, edited by Christopher Coyne and Rachel Coyne, 29–44. London: Institute of Economic Affairs.

Rigbi, Oren. 2013. "The Effects of Usury Laws: Evidence from the Online Loan Market." *Review of Economics and Statistics* 95 (4): 1238–48.

Rougeau, Vincent D. 1996. "Rediscovering Usury: An Argument for Legal Controls on Credit Card Interest Rates." *University of Colorado Law Review* 67 (1): 1–46.

Schmidtz, David. 2016. "Are Price Controls Fair?" *Supreme Court Economic Review* 23 (1): 221–33.

Schuettinger, Robert L., and Eamonn F. Butler. 1979. *Forty Centuries of Wage and Price Controls: How Not to Fight Inflation*. Washington DC: Heritage Foundation.

Siebert, W. Stanley. 2015. "The Simple Economics of Wage Floors." In *Flaws and Ceilings: Price Controls and the Damage They Cause*, edited by Christopher Coyne and Rachel Coyne, 45–71. London: Institute of Economic Affairs.

Smith, Adam. 1776. *The Wealth of Nations*. The Electric Book Co.

Snowdon, Christopher. 2015. "Minimum Unit Pricing." In *Flaws and Ceilings: Price Controls and the Damage They Cause*, edited by Christopher Coyne and Rachel Coyne, 177–97. London: Institute of Economic Affairs.
Sowell, Thomas. 1980. *Knowledge and Decisions*. New York: Basic Books.
Tabakoğlu, Ahmet. 2016. *İslam İktisadına Giriş* [An Introduction to Islamic Economics]. İstanbul: Dergah Yayınları.
Vandenbrink, Donna. 1982. "The Effects of Usury Ceilings." *Economic Perspectives* 6 (1): 44–55.
Wellings, Richard. 2015. "Regulation of Rail Fares." In *Flaws and Ceilings: Price Controls and the Damage They Cause*, edited by Christopher Coyne and Rachel Coyne, 118–34. London: Institute of Economic Affairs.

CHAPTER 6

Basics of Islamic Economics and the Prohibition of Riba

An economic system is the way of organization of production, distribution, and consumption of goods and services by individuals, establishments, and governments. It is possible to classify economic systems in various ways. However, the most cited classification of economic systems is the one that is made with regard to the level of the relative effectiveness of the markets and governments in economics-related decision-making. According to their way of deciding what and how to produce and how to allocate the output, the systems are defined as a traditional, market, mixed market, mixed socialist, or planned economies (Askari et al. 2015).

Islam emerged in a society, which highly benefited from an economic system that was mainly based on trade (Hamidullah 1980). Arabs had a well-organized trade system operating on an enormous route between Europe, India, China, and Korea, with huge caravans up to 2500 camels. Trade was not a big business only in the length of the routes and size of the exchanges, but it was complicated in many aspects, such that Arabs were considered the inventors of world trade (Koehler 2014).

By the emergence and prevalence of Islamic belief, the merchants modified some rules of economic activities according to Islamic principles, but the trade-based economics system went on performing actively. Although Schumpeter (1986), one of the most prominent intellectuals of the twentieth-century in economics, claimed that almost nothing produced relevant to economic thought in the five centuries until the

C. Eyerci, *The Causes and Consequences of Interest Theory*,
https://doi.org/10.1007/978-3-030-78702-8_6

thirteenth century, in the "great gap" as he called, it was not the case in the Muslim world. Many Muslim scholars worked on economics-related issues and contributed to the economic thought with an Islamic perspective in the mentioned period (Ghazanfar and Islahi 2003). From the seventh to the fifteenth-century, the Muslim world, in the region from Spain to Central and South Asia, benefited from one of the world's largest and most prosperous market economies. The economy, which mainly grounded on long-distance trade, benefited from a stable currency of gold and silver and yielded many innovations such as bills of exchange, limited partnerships, and checks (Grassie 2010).

Muslim scholars of various disciplines, such as jurists, historians, and philosophers, continued exerting on economic thought until the fifteenth century but at a decreasing intensity. Then, thought disappeared almost in all fields, including economics in the Muslim world for centuries (Chapra 2000).

The reemergence of Islamic economic thought as *Islamic economics* (Grassie 2010) is after the Second World War. While Muslim countries were constructing their economies after independence, the Islamic approach of economics began to reappear (Chapra 2000). During the last few decades, applications of Islamic economics, specifically in finance and insurance, became prevalent in Muslim countries. The financial sectors in Muslim and non-Muslim countries as well were motivated to develop interest-free instruments following the capital owners' preferences by the attraction of the accumulated capital in Muslim countries (Cohen 2017). In consequence, although its share in total world financial assets is still about 1%, Islamic finance assets have grown from $1.22 trillion in 2012 (Cohen 2017) to $2.44 trillion in 2017, almost at an annual rate of 15%. According to an estimation, Islamic finance assets will reach a volume of $3.81 trillion in 2023 (Thomson Reuters 2018).

Among other systems, Islamic economics is considered distinct by many Muslim scholars (Khan 2013). The distinction was manifested in the definitions of Islamic economics made by scholars (Hasanuzzaman 1984; Khan 1984; Arif 1985; Haneef 2005; Hasan 2016) in various ways (Chapra 1996; Kahf 2014). However, almost all assertions commonly focused on the fact that the economic activities are guided not only by the desires and experiences of humans but also by the basic principles of Islamic law in Islamic economics (Azid 2010).

The role of institutions in reducing uncertainty and lowering transaction costs is considered highly important (North 1991) because, since

Coase, it has been accepted that the transaction costs are the main obstacle for economic growth (Karayiannis and Hatzis 2010). Similar to other systems, institutions such as property rights, contracts, trust, markets, wealth accumulation and utilization, business ethics, and competition and cooperation are also taking place in Islamic economics with some distinctive features mainly aiming to attain social justice (Askari et al. 2015).

In the first section of this chapter, the basic principles of the Islamic economic system that differ from the conventional ones are briefly presented.

The relevant issues to the prohibition of interest are reviewed in the second section. The pre-Islamic riba is introduced, and the origins of the ban in *the Quran* (holy book) and *Sunnah* (practices of the Prophet) are briefed. Finally, the approach of *fiqh* (Islamic jurisprudence) to riba and interest is shortly reviewed, and the traditional view is presented.

In the next section, some of the opposing views to the traditional approach are summarized. The fourth section is on the instruments alternatively developed to interest-based transactions and other devious ways used to overcome the prohibition of interest.

A chronological bibliography of Islamic economics on the concept of interest is attached in Appendix 6.1.

6.1 The Basics of Islamic Economic System

The collection of the economic practices of Muslims, which were modified from time to time in line with the changes in Islamic economic thought during more than a millennium, was called *Islamic economics* afterward.

The basic principles grounding on the Quran and Sunnah are constructing the Islamic economic system and differentiating it from the conventional ones. Therefore, it is essential to note that a considerable part of the content of Islamic economics is normative (Khan 1994; Zarqa 2003; Haneef and Furqani 2011). Accordingly, the assertions of Islamic economists are mostly about desirable ideals, and it is hard to talk about a positive approach within the system. In this context, various institutions emerged in the Islamic economic system. Some principals that characterize the main features of the system are enumerated below.

The first principle is to maintain the efficiency of the free market. That means, Islamic economics, mostly a market-based system, considers the market as the most efficient organization in the distribution of the resources in production and consumption. However, the efficiency of markets requires the protection of the parties such as employees, entrepreneurs, investors, and customers by rules and enforcement mechanisms (Askari et al. 2015).

It can be said that *social justice* is one of the foremost objectives of Islamic economics (Azid 2010). A just society requires economic justice, and for economic justice, there should be equality in opportunity for all members of the community. That implies equal access to resources such as natural resources, education, and technology. Secondly, the system requires justice in exchange to protect parties of any transaction. Finally, a just distribution is essential for economic justice. Equality in opportunity can provide balance in the distribution of wealth that is earned by people's efforts and abilities using their labor or capital. However, the Islamic approach aims to secure justice in the allocation of transferred and inherited wealth from its producers (Askari et al. 2015). Muslim wealth holders have to pay a wealth tax, *zakat* that is 2.5% of the liquid accumulated wealth, and various rates for wealth in other forms (Choudhury and Malik 1992). Moreover, people are encouraged to help needy people by transferring some wealth to them in various ways. On the other hand, Islam defined the cannons of inheritance in detail.

Risk-sharing became a more prevalent and effective organizational form in Islamic economics compared to the conventional economic systems by the prohibition of all types of interest-based transactions. It is expected that risk-sharing would distribute the risk among all relevant parties in the market instead of burdening the risk on the borrowers only (Choudhury and Malik 1992). On the income side, the absence of interest-based transactions gives rise to the cooperation of entrepreneurs and investors through *profit-sharing* (Choudhury and Malik 1992). A relevant issue is the existence of the debt. Since some scholars consider debt to be unjust, a tool of exploitation, and a source of inequality, according to them, the debt-based economy is not legitimated in Islamic economics (Azid 2010).

The role of the state is regarded as inevitable in achieving social justice in the traditional Islamic approach. A country should ensure compliance with the principles of social and economic justice. To fulfill this requirement, the state (Askari et al. 2015).

- realizes the equality in opportunity for everybody in access to resources,
- supervises and enforces the markets to maintain justice in exchange,
- coordinates the transfers to the needy people and administers the implementation of inheritance laws for the sake of distributive justice that is considered vital in fighting against poverty,
- above all, guarantees the existence and operability of the judicial system and the costless accessibility of each member of the society to it.

6.2 Prohibition of Interest

As being, presumably, the most significant reason that distinguishes Islamic economics from the conventional ones, the prohibition of interest or riba, as it is originally called, has always attracted attention and has been studied in many aspects thoroughly. It should be stated in advance that undoubtedly, the Muslim scholars agreed on the explicit prohibition of riba (Khan 2013) both in the Quran and in Sunnah. The controversy is about the meaning and nature of riba (Z. Ahmad 1978; Farooq 2007). Riba means increment, rise, addition, expansion, or growth (Uludağ 1988; Chapra 2006), and it is defined to be a source of injustice, economic illness, an obstacle for spirituality, and a threat to welfare (DeLorenzo 2006). More specifically, it is claimed that riba

- is exploitive (Chapra 2006),
- worsens the gap of wealth distribution,
- causes a tendency to inflation,
- is an unjust income,
- causes to discount the future,
- causes economic volatility,
- harms the motivation of entrepreneurship (Lawal 2016),
- corrupts society,
- causes negative growth,
- diminishes human personality (Siddiqi 2004).

Before reviewing the grounds of the ban, an introduction to the historical development of practicing riba in the pre-Islamic period would be informative.

6.2.1 *The Pre-Islamic Riba*

When it was prohibited in the seventh century, riba was not a newly developed instrument in the part of the world that Muslims have been living. It was an old on-going pre-Islamic practice. While banning, it was not defined because the prohibited action was known well (Z. Ahmad 1978). *Riba al-jahiliyyah*, as it is called afterward, was the exorbitant increment in the debt, doubling or tripling, for example, when it was not paid on the date of maturity (Uludağ 1988). The origin of the debt might be a borrowed loan or another liability due to a previously buying for an account or a similar transaction (Gül 2017). However, regarding the borrowed loan, the method of lending at the beginning is highly controversial (S. Ahmad 2007). According to some scholars, lending was being made free of interest for the first term. However, others claimed that the first lending was also being made at interest. In the case of default, predetermined interest was increasing (Rahman 1964). The pre-Islamic riba, at least the mostly referred component of it, was the same as today's penalty for delay or interest of default. In other words, it was different from credit interest (Z. Ahmad 1978).

On the other hand, regarding riba, it is argued that there was not a predetermined reasonable increment rate by an authority or the market, and the co-determinants of the increment were the severity of the debtor's needs and the fairness of the claimant (Erdem 2018). Although there were reports on some debts originated from the borrowing of merchants, who used the capital in trade, the debtors were mostly the needy people (Gül 2017). As might be expected, the practice was causing inevitable troubles and misery for the needy people who borrowed for indispensable reasons (Z. Ahmad 1978).

6.2.2 *Riba in Quran*

By the methodology of the Quran's gradual approach for the adaptation of the society (Erdem 2018), it did not prohibit riba instantly; instead, extending over time, the verses first implied riba's negativities, then condemned practicing it, and finally banned it explicitly.

Chronologically, the first verse in the Quran concerning riba (sure 30, verse 39) declares that loans given at riba for an increment in possessions are not of value in the sight of God, but instead praises giving in charity. The following relevant verses (sure 4, verses 160–161) are recalling how the previous societies, specifically Jews, were treated due to receiving riba that was banned. However, the verse did not yet prohibit it.

The prohibition of riba is clearly stated afterward, by explicitly decreeing not to take the folded riba, referring to the pre-Islamic practice (sure 3, verse 130). Another verse (sure 2, verse 275) replied the ones considering trade to be the same as riba by stressing that trade is licit, but riba is illicit. Finally, the Quran ordered the believers to give up the riba that was not yet received (sure 2, verse 278).

The following verses of the abovementioned three ones inform about awards for respecting prohibition, such as mercy of God and divine gift, and about punishments for receiving riba, such as being sent to hell. Receiving riba is defined as fighting against God and the Prophet. The current lenders are ordered to grant a delay to the borrowers that are in trouble and favorably recommended to renounce for the reason that it would be more propitious for them.

6.2.3 Riba in Sunnah

Riba in Sunnah appears in several *hadiths* (the statements, actions, and approvals of the Prophet). Some of the hadiths did not decree on riba but discredited and condemned it by informing about its moral and religious consequences. Within the last sermon in Mecca, the Prophet recalled the decree of the Quran regarding the abolition of pre-Islamic riba (Chapra 2006). Before this, in many other hadiths, he declared that (Uludağ 1988).

- Riba is a big sin,
- The parties of a riba transaction, its witnesses and registrars as well, are damned,
- All the yield from riba will be lost soon,
- When riba becomes prevalent in a society, that society deserves to be punished,
- Insisting on practicing riba is similar to being an idolater, etc.

Some other hadiths were not explicitly about the evilness of riba, but these praised giving alms, aiding, easing debt, and similar alternatives of riba (Uludağ 1988):

- The aid made for God's sake is multiplied in the sight of God,
- The ones who aid without taunting will neither worry nor sorrow,
- The help made for God's sake is actually for the aider himself,
- Postponing the loan of the borrower that is in trouble until he eases is advised. Renouncing the loan is more propitious for the lender,
- The lender who wants God to alleviate her problems on the Day of Judgment shall ease her borrower or discount the loan, etc.

The third group of hadiths described riba in addition to the description in the Quran (Uludağ 1988;Chapra 2006). Some hadiths in this group were about commercial transactions. A widely cited hadith is about the trade of some commodities. Such trade-relevant hadiths were informing that.

- The products, gold, silver, wheat, barley, date, and salt can be exchanged in kind but at the same quantity and not deferring. Any excess on one side is defined to be riba,
- On the other hand, trading two different commodities of any amounts is licit but only if it is a spot transaction,
- There is no riba in spot selling and buying,
- Deferred livestock trade is not prohibited, etc.

The remaining hadiths of the third group were about the loans at riba, mentioning the issues of (Chapra 2006).

- Any benefit yielding from a loan is riba,
- The lender shall not accept any gift from the borrower,
- There is no riba except in deferred transactions, etc.

Sunnah is highly crucial as evidence for Islamic jurisprudence, but of course, in being evidence, it was not considered as absolute as the Quran. Thus, concerning its extent and interpretation, Sunnah was variously approached by Muslim jurists (Z. Ahmad 1978). Furthermore, the reliability of some hadiths on riba is not satisfactory enough. While some of these are reported to be authentic, there are also weak ones. Even some widely known as fabricated ones are cited in riba literature. On the other hand, although reliable hadiths are used as evidence in decreeing on riba by most of the jurists, due to being *khabar al-vahid* (report of one person), they are not considered to be absolute evidence in economics by some other jurists (Uludağ 1988).

6.2.4 *Riba in Fiqh (Islamic Jurisprudence) and the Traditional Perspective*

As mentioned above, there was no doubt that the pre-Islamic riba was prohibited in Islam. However, the thought of jurists on the scope of riba that mentioned in the Quran and Sunnah were diversified. The differences were not only about the conception of the hadiths. Differences in methodologies of the jurists in making analogies resulted in the emergence of various decrees for the same issue.

An analogy requires defining the cause of the existing decree, which might be a verse or hadith. The differences in the specified causes by the jurists were another source of diversification. Unfortunately, the cause of the prohibition of riba was one of the highly debated issues in Islamic Jurisprudence, and expectedly, it was not agreed on (Deniz 2006). For example, the abovementioned hadith about the prohibition of the exchange of six commodities in kind with an excess interpreted variously by different schools and scholars (Uludağ 1988).

A group asserted that the prohibition of exchange in kind with excess was valid for any commodity similar to these six ones. A subgroup defined the similarity according to the commodity's measurement unit. All products measured in weight as gold and silver were similar to gold and silver, and the commodities measured in volume as the other four products were decreed as those four. Other products that were not measured in weight or volume, but measured in number, length, or area were not in the scope of the prohibition.

Another subgroup excluded gold and silver from any analogy and kept apart, but considering the remained four commodities were food products, defined all foodstuffs to be in the scope of the prohibition.

A third subgroup agreed with the former approach but limited the scope with the storable foods and excluded the perishables. There were several further considerations of the hadith in this group, which differentiate in detail.

On the other hand, some others approached the issue distinctly and claimed that the prohibition was exclusively for the mentioned six commodities. Any other good was not subject to the ban.

As it is exemplified, the variety in the interpretation of riba was observed, more or less, for many other relevant issues. The divergence of the jurists on the riba-related matters in detail, and sometimes in basics, is plausible to some extent. Even so, in some cases, ampleness of divergence prevents concluding prohibition of riba with a mind at peace. Specifically, the challenges of modern times deepen the trouble in the conception of riba. Therefore, the need for continuous clarification of the interpretations, in compliance with the ever-changing world and conditions is increasing.

Despite the existence of different approaches, the most common interpretation of the evidence in the Quran and Sunnah dominated others, and a mainstream thought on riba emerged. According to the mentioned most common interpretation that became the traditional view of Islam afterward, *riba is the addition to the principal that is paid by the borrower to the lender for either the loan or an extension in the loan's maturity* (Chapra 2006). The prohibited riba has some specifications (Askari et al. 2015):

- Its rate is defined in advance and higher than zero,
- It is valid for an amount of loan for a fixed term,
- Its payment does not depend on the success or profitability of the activity for which the loan used,
- An authority enforces its payment.

This traditional definition regards riba just the same as the interest in conventional economics. Within this frame, any form of interest is not allowed:

- Whatever its type, simple or compound interest,
- Whatever its rate, low or high,
- Whoever it is paid by, poor or wealthy people,
- However it is arisen, from a credit or deposit,
- Whatever the purpose of loan it is paid for, consumption or production,
- Wherever it is practiced, in lending or trade.

Although the traditional view was highly dominant and received wide acceptance, there have always been alternative views on the nature of riba.

6.3 Contrarians of the Traditional Perspective on Interest

The approaches of mainstream scholars that formed the traditional view on riba were, actually, not uniform. There were many minor and some more considerable distinctions among the assertions of the scholars in the mainstream approach. However, there have also been other scholars who differed from the traditional approach regarding major issues (Farooq 2007). There are also some contemporary Islamic economists asserting diversified thoughts similar to the older contrarians (Kamla and Alsoufi 2015). A brief review of some of those scholars' arguments in the following would exhibit how the view on interest in Islam is diversified.

Abdullah ibn Abbas, one of the Prophet's cousins, is among the first contrarians of the conventional view. He asserted that the prohibition was only for the pre-Islamic riba, and interest on commercial transactions could not be regarded as in the scope of the ban. A fourteenth-century prominent jurist, Ibn Qayyim's thought was similar to Abdullah ibn Abbas. However, he also claimed that the prohibition of interest in commercial transactions was implicitly made to prevent the tendency to pre-Islamic riba (Khalil 2006).

Zayd ibn Ali, the great-grandson of Prophet and an eminent jurist of the eighth century, allowed the difference between the forward and spot prices of a good in exchange. Such a contract was valid as long as there was a mutual consent of the seller and the buyer. The amount of the difference depends on the length of the time passed from the sale to the payment. An asset received without paying at sale time is productive that may be benefited or used in trade (Siddiqi 1982).

Sir Syed Ahmed Khan was one of the contrarians of the traditional view in the nineteenth century. According to him, the prohibited riba was only about the loans given to needy people at an excessive rate of interest. The interest on the loans borrowed by wealthy people and the interest received from the bank deposits were not prohibited. After a few decades, Mulana Iqbal Ahmed, one of the initiators of the Saud Mand Movement, asserted that not all increments were riba. The prohibited riba was the increment due to a default of a debt that arose from a deferred sale (Aziz et al. 2008).

At the beginning of the twentieth century, Muhammad Abduh, scholar and the mufti, the highest religious authority of Egypt, declared that the interest received from the saving deposits was legitimate. However, some others asserted that Abduh's permission was valid only if the savings were utilized under the rules of mudarabah. Following him, his student Rashid Rida defined the prohibited riba as the compound interest. Ahmad Al Sanhuri was another dissented jurist who was active in the midst of the century. He considered the pre-Islamic riba as the only directly prohibited interest and equated it with modern compound interest. According to him, the prohibition of other types of interest was to reduce the tendency to prohibited riba. Thus, the pre-Islamic riba could be permitted only for acute necessities, but different types of interest may be received in case of a slight need (Khalil and Thomas 2006).

Another contrarian of the early twentieth century was the Turkish scholar İzmirli İsmail Hakkı. He claimed that the prohibited riba was the pre-Islamic riba that is just like the folded debt due to default, as it is worded in the Quran (Uludağ 1988).

Among many others, Fazlur Rahman (1964) has been, presumably, the most cited scholar, regarding his view of the distinction between riba and interest. After reviewing riba-relevant hadiths in various aspects along with Quran, he concluded that the prohibited riba is the exorbitant increment in loan due to a postponement of its payment date, and this has to be prevented by the use of the law. According to him, the prohibition was expanded in the hadith literature. The inconsistencies within the literature caused the rigidity of the ban to increase. He stated that the alternative of riba is sadaqah, a form of cooperation and mutual consideration of individuals, and this would help to overcome the problem with riba. However, unless society practices a sadaqah based system efficiently, abolishing interest would undermine the economic welfare of society. He asserted, on the other hand, that in an economy where wealth and capital increase to the point that supply of and demand for capital are nearly equalized, the interest rate would decrease almost to zero, but such an economic development requires the existence of higher interest rates.

A contemporary example was the approach of Muhammad Sayyid Tantawi, another mufti of Egypt. In 1989, he announced that the interest-bearing financial instruments beneficial for each party of the transaction were religiously allowed (Grassie 2010).

Imad-ad-Dean Ahmad (1996) asserted that the term riba in the Quran explicitly means usury, and it was practiced by receiving an excessive interest from the needy borrowers. According to him, the scope of riba was extended by hadith to all types of exchanges made at exorbitant prices. He referred to the legitimacy of the difference between the spot and forward prices in a sale as the evidence for interest not being the same as riba. Ahmad also raised the issue of depreciation of loaned money due to inflation, and he claimed that any loss in value of a loan is unfair and not acceptable according to principles of the Quran.

Maha-Hanaan Balala (2011) stressed the crucial issue that the Quran stated the importance of efficiency and equity in the market, and any decree could not contradict these principles. She asserted that there is no evidence in the Quran and hadiths to consider all the interest-based transactions as riba. According to her, interest in non-commercial operations is prohibited, and commercial lending at a just interest rate determined by the market is allowed.

Ugi Suharto (2018) asserted that some types of interest could not be considered riba. The difference between the present and future prices is interest and legitimate in Islam. Although the difference is not defined as interest, the existence of the instruments based on forward- sale used by Islamic finance institutions proves that such practices are not prohibited. He claimed that it is not right to define Islamic finance as an interest-free financial system. Instead, he proposed to call it *riba-free banking and finance*.

Rauf Azhar (2019) scrutinized the prohibition of riba in his book of 2010 and redefined riba as the folded increase in debt in the case of default. He stated that, in this aspect, riba is neither interest nor usury.

Lastly, presumably the most comprehensive approach, apart from the traditional view, was brought by Muhammad Akram Khan. In his book (Khan 2013) that was introduced by himself as an effort to depart from the mainstream thought, the concept of Islamic economics was reviewed, evaluated, and explicitly criticized in almost all aspects. Then, Khan (2020) proposed a definition for riba as the increment in (i) loans given to poor people, (ii) loans given to friends, relatives, neighbors, and colleagues in a social context, and (iii) the debt as the penalty of the case of default. Following the definition, he listed the transactions that are not prohibited:

- Difference between the forward and spot price in a sale transaction,
- Penalty for delayed debt payment for the first time,
- Lending at interest for production purposes,
- Interest paid for deposits,
- Loan interest not more than the loss in the real value of the principal,
- Extra payment made by the debtor voluntarily as a gift or similar,

- Using interest in discounting within project evaluation and budgeting,
- Voluntary reduction by the lender due to early repayment of a loan,
- Reduction in the principal not more than the rate of deflation,
- Voluntary reduction in the principal by the lender as a gift or similar,
- Increase or decrease in repayment voluntarily made by the debtor for the changed quality of the loaned item,
- Revaluation of the loaned principal with the agreement of the debtor and the lender, due to changes in the market price of a product or exchange rate.

The divergent views from the mainstream concept of riba and the scholars that asserted these views are summarized in Table 6.1.

Even though the supporters of the traditional view have a vast majority, the agreement on the equivalence of riba and interest is not observed dominantly in all cases. Scrutinizing various translations of the term *riba* in the Quran into English gives an idea of the perceptions or considerations of the translators regarding the meaning of riba. The word *riba*, with its conceptual meaning relevant to economics, is used eight times in six verses of four sures in the Quran. As it is itemized in Table 6.7 in Appendix 6.2, 19 translations of the Quran into English (*Hasenat Quranic Research Application* (version 6.1) 2015), including almost all eminent translations, the word *riba* was translated as *interest* 35 times, but as *usury* 111 times (Table 6.2). The word *interest* was used alone 14 times and used in a group with *riba*, *usury*, and other words 21 times. Since *interest* is considered to have the most comprehensive and inclusive coverage in meaning, whether it is used alone or with other words, both translations must be regarded to mention *interest*.

The term in verse (sure 3, verse 130) by which the prohibition of riba explicitly stated is translated into *usury* by 15 translators and into *interest* by four translators only. On the other hand, 14 translators used the word *usury* more than four times, while four translators used the word *interest* more than four times in their translations (Table 6.3).

Whether following the traditional view or not, the approaches of the scholars worked on riba and interest were classified by Süleyman Uludağ (1988) in four groups concerning their perception of the issue (Table 6.4). The first group supports the prevailing view that is objecting to riba and interest on one hand, but on the other hand, implicitly legitimates interest by permitting some devious instruments used to evade the prohibition. The second group considers riba and interest to be the same, explicitly refuses both of them, and regards any dishonest way to be

Table 6.1 The views contrary to the traditional concept of Riba

Divergent view	*Scholars that asserted the view*
Only the folded increase in defaulted debt, namely the pre-Islamic riba, is prohibited	Abdullah ibn Abbas (seventh century) Ahmad Al Sanhuri (twentieth century) İzmirli İsmail Hakkı (twentieth century) Fazlur Rahman (twentieth century) Rauf Azhar (twenty-first century) Muhammad Akram Khan (twenty-first century)
Interest on commercial transactions is not riba	Abdullah ibn Abbas (seventh century) Ibn Qayyim (fourteenth century) Maha-Hanaan Balala (twenty-first century)
The difference between the forward and spot prices of a good is not riba	Zayd ibn Ali (eighth century)
The interest on the loans borrowed by wealthy people and the interest received from the bank deposits	Sir Syed Ahmed Khan (nineteenth century)
The prohibited riba was the increment due to a default of a debt that arose from a deferred sale	Mulana Iqbal Ahmed (nineteenth century)
Interest received from the saving deposits is legitimate	Muhammad Abduh (twentieth century)
Prohibited riba as the compound interest	Rashid Rida (twentieth century)
Interest-bearing financial instruments beneficial for each party are legitimate	Muhammad Sayyid Tantawi (twentieth century)
Excessive interest received from the needy borrowers is prohibited	Imad-ad-Dean Ahmad (twentieth century)
The depreciation of loaned money due to inflation is unfair and not acceptable according to Islamic principles	Imad-ad-Dean Ahmad (twentieth century)
Interest on loans given to poor people is prohibited	Muhammad Akram Khan (twenty-first century)
Interest on loans given to friends, relatives, neighbors, and colleagues in a social context is prohibited	Muhammad Akram Khan (twenty-first century)

illicit. The third and fourth groups allow interest, but they severely object to riba by considering it as usury. The third group stays in the frame of fiqh, the Islamic jurisprudence, but allows interest by glossing the relevant decrees. The last group does not remain within the scope of fiqh and allows interest by reevaluating the verses of the Quran and relevant hadiths.

Table 6.2 The words used for Riba in nineteen translations of Quran into English, by verse *(frequency)*

Sure: Verse	*Translated as*					
	Interest		*Riba*	*Usury*	*Others*	*Total*
	Interest alone	*with Riba, Usury or other words*				
2:275-a	3	3		13		19
2:275-b	2	2	1	14		19
2:275-c	3	1	1	14		19
2:276	1	3		15		19
2:278	2	2	1	14		19
3:130	1	3		15		19
4:161		4		15		19
30:39	2	3		11	3	19
Total	14	21	3	111	3	152

6.4 The Alternative Instruments to Interest and Devious Ways

In the absence of interest-based transactions in Muslim societies, on the one hand, the alternative ways of capital utilization in investment advanced, and on the other hand, some alternative instruments used in lending emerged. Some of the methods and apparatus are still used in the Islamic financial sector.

The alternative lending instruments were mostly used to evade the prohibition of interest. These instruments were not wholly allowed and supported by all jurists of the traditional approach. Some scholars defined them as cheating. Moreover, it was claimed that the interest rates of loans in such devious instruments might be well above the rates of explicit interest-based lending (Uludağ 1988). However, a considerable number of scholars legitimate them. In consequence, these instruments are commonly in use.

In the meanwhile, although *qarz e hasna*, the interest-free loan given for charitable purposes, has been widely mentioned within this frame, it is not an alternative to interest-based transactions, and not realistic, particularly in large-scale commercial lending.

Table 6.3 The words used for *Riba* in nineteen translations of Quran into English, by translator *(frequency)*

Translator	*Translated as*					
	Interest		*Riba*	*Usury*	*Others*	*Total*
	Interest alone	*with Riba, Usury or other words*				
Abdul Majid Daryabadi				7	1	8
Abdullah Yusuf Ali				7	1	8
Ali Quli Qara				8		8
Amatul Rahman Omar	1	7				8
Faridul Haque				8		8
Hajj Abdalhaq and Aisha Bewley				8		8
Hamid S. Aziz				8		8
IFTA Committee				8		8
M. Hilali and Muhsin Khan				7	1	8
M. J. Ahmed and Samira Ahmed		8				8
Muhammad Abdel Haleem				8		8

(continued)

Table 6.3 (continued)

Translator	*Translated as*					
	Interest		*Riba*	*Usury*	*Others*	*Total*
	Interest alone	*with Riba, Usury or other words*				
Muhammad Asad				8		8
Muhammad Habib Shakir				8		8
Muhammad Mahmud Ghali		5	3			8
Muhammad Marmaduke Pickthall				8		8
Sheikh Muhammad Sarwar	7			1		8
Syed Vickar Ahamed	2	1		5		8
Thomas B. Irving	4			4		8
Wahiduddin Khan				8		8
Total	14	21	3	111	3	152

Table 6.4 The four groups of Muslim scholars' consideration of Riba and interest

In theory	*Is interest allowed?*	*How is it allowed?*
Riba and interest are the same and prohibited	Yes	By permitting devious instruments
	No	–
Riba is prohibited, but some types of interest are legitimate	Yes	By glossing the relevant decrees in the frame of fiqh
	Yes	By reevaluating the verses of the Quran and relevant hadiths

Source Uludağ (1988)

6.4.1 *Profit-Loss Sharing Instruments*

Among several contract types, ***mudaraba*** and ***musharaka*** (Askari et al. 2015) are the most mentioned models based on profit-loss sharing. Although there are concerns about their efficiency in various aspects (Khan 2013), there is almost no objection to the legitimacy of these models.

Mudaraba operates by the partnership of an investor and an entrepreneur. The investor is the capital owner, and the entrepreneur is a specialized agent in the operations of the invested real sector. The contract of mudaraba is usually made for a limited time. At the end of the term, the profit is shared according to the agreement within the contract.

A similar partnership model, musharaka, provides the partnership of two or more parties who gather their capital and labor, if they want, with the same rights and liabilities. The profit is shared according to their agreement at the beginning. However, any loss is shared in the proportion of each partner's capital in the total investment.

6.4.2 *Sale with a Promise to Repurchase*

An owner of a property, who needs to borrow, sells her property to a capital owner with an agreement to repurchase it for the same price at a predetermined date. The buyer of the property rents it to the seller, and the seller continues to use it by paying a monthly rent. At the predetermined time, the property is sold back, and the capital owner receives the price he previously paid to buy the property. The monthly-received rent is the profit of the capital invested, similar to the interest of a loan.

When the repurchase of the property is guaranteed, and a previously determined repurchasing price is used rather than the market price at the transaction date, the process is just the same as lending money at an interest that is equal to the rental of the property. The rental, namely interest, may be received at predetermined intervals or once at the end of the rental, namely loan, period. The selling price of the property is equal to the repurchasing price that is the same as paying the loaned principal back at the end of the loan period.

6.4.3 Sale of the Right of Use

Ijara, an instrument similar to *leasing* in conventional economics, is the sale of the right of use of a good for a previously determined period. Although it became a financial instrument, it was a trading model in Muslim countries at the beginning. In ijara transaction, the lesser buys and rents an asset to the demander, while holding the maintenance and insurance responsibilities of the asset. The parties negotiate the terms of the transaction at pre-agreed dates to keep the rental in line with the market rates.

In another model similar to ijara, namely *hire-purchase*, the lessee has the opportunity to buy the asset after the compilation of the rent period. This time, the applied rental fee includes both the actual rental and the deferred price of the asset. When the planned payment is completed, possession of the asset is transferred from the lesser to the lessee (Mirakhor and Zaidi 2007).

6.4.4 Instruments Based on Forward Sale

Salam is a contract of exchange based on forward sale. In this model, the buyer makes the payment in advance but receives the goods bought in the future. The farmers, who are financially in trouble, may sell their crops that not grew yet, a few months in advance. The merchants pay the price of the crops cheaper than the probable price of the crops at harvest time (Uludağ 1988). The difference in price is, no doubt, an interest determined due to the time between the payment date and expected harvest date. It is not surprising to observe severe troubles in the case of the farmers' such that the implicit rate of interest tends to increase to usurious levels.

Delivering a good at present and receiving its payment in the future is an exchange model that is the reverse of salam. In general, the forward price of the good is higher than its spot price. The difference between spot and forward prices, this once, depends on the time passed from the delivery date to payment date (Uludağ 1988).

The forward sale is not only an instrument of trading. It is widely used in various ways in lending contracts. In a direct model, a borrower buys an item at a forward price of $120, for example. She becomes indebted to the seller of the item. The loan will be paid back at the agreed date in the future. Then, the borrower sells the item back in the market at a spot price of $100. Sometimes, the item is sold at a lower price due to the urgency of need.

In a transaction called *double sale*, a lender sells an item to a borrower at a $120 forward price to be paid one year later, for example. The borrower sells the item she bought back to the lender at a spot price of $100, and the lender pays $100 to the borrower. Now, the borrower has a debt of $120 that is the borrowed $100 at a 20% interest rate, to be paid one year later (Khalil 2006).

In a *triple sale* model, like in double sale, a lender sells an item to a borrower at a $120 forward price to be paid one year later, but this time the borrower does not sell the item directly back to the lender. Instead, it is sold to a third party at a spot price of $100. Then, the new buyer sells it to the lender, who is the first seller of the item for $100. Thus, the third party receives nothing in net, and the borrower has a debt of $120 again, to be paid one year later.

Several alternative models are using forward sales. As a final example, a lender lends $100 free of interest for one year; besides, she sells a pencil to the borrower at a $20 of forward price to be paid again one year later. The actual transaction is the same as the previous models: a debt of $120 due to a $100 loan at 20% interest rate (Uludağ 1988).

Today, *Murabahah*, which is based on forward sale, is the most widely used financial instrument by Islamic financial institutions. Within a murabahah transaction, the lender sells an item on credit to the borrower at a price that is equal to the sum of the item's present cost and a profit. In murabahah, differently from the conventional forward sale, the lending institution has to inform the borrower about the cost price of the item and the rate of profit (Khan 2013).

However, some scholars regard the utilization of the difference between the forward and spot prices in this way as charging interest by indexing the time-value of money (Al-Masri 2004; Grassie 2010).

The processes of some instruments used as alternatives to interest are summarized in Table 6.5.

Table 6.5 Some instruments used in Islamic economics alternative to interest

Principle used	*Process in brief*
Profit-loss sharing	The partners share the profit or loss considering the capital, entrepreneurship, and labor used, i.e., ***mudaraba, musharaka***
Sale with a promise to repurchase	The borrower sells a property to the lender, hires it, pays rent, and repurchases
Sale of the right of use	The borrower pays a rental fee and the deferred price of an asset until clearing the debt, i.e., ***ijara***
Forward sale	The farmers sell their crops that not grew yet at a price lower than their price at harvest, i.e., ***salam***
	The buyer receives an item at present and pays for it in the future at a price higher than its spot price
	The borrower buys an item at a forward price and sells it back in the market at spot price or lower
	The borrower buys an item at a forward price from the lender and sells it back to the lender at spot price, i.e., ***double sale***
	The borrower buys an item at a forward price from the lender, sells it to a third party at spot price, and the new buyer sells it to the lender at the same price she bought, i.e., ***triple sale***
	The borrower buys an item on credit from the lender at a price that is equal to the sum of the item's present cost and a profit, i.e., ***murabahah***

6.4.5 *Cash Waqfs*

Despite its prohibition, there had been illegal lending at interest in the Muslim world (Calder 2016), and the interest rate for illicit loans had been usuriously high. It was reported that in the Ottoman Empire in the sixteenth century, there was illegal lending up to an annual interest rate of 50%. Even in a case, 30% monthly, that 360% yearly rate of interest was observed. The allowed annual rate with legal instruments, including for the loans of the cash waqfs, was 15% (Uludağ 1988). In Istanbul, in the seventeenth and eighteenth centuries, the allowed interest rate of lending was changing in a range of 15–20%, and the interest rate of the loans of the waqfs was four percentage points lower than the interest rate in the lending of the non-waqf lenders at an average (Kuran and Rubin 2017).

The *cash waqf* was another instrument used in lending, particularly in the Ottoman Empire. The waqfs, namely the trusts established for various charitable purposes, were being actively operated since the beginning in Muslim societies. In general, the endowed assets were real properties and the movables that accompanied those properties. However, in the eighth century, the legitimacy of the establishment of waqfs by donating money had been widely discussed. Although a consensus on the issue was not achieved, some scholars of the Hanafi school of Islamic Jurisprudence legitimated the establishment of cash waqfs based on the endowment of money (Dumlu 2015). The cash waqfs were considered to protect ordinary borrowers from the usurious interest rates of other lenders (Bulut and Korkut 2017) like a loan market stabilizer.

The cash waqfs became prevalent in the Ottoman Empire in the fifteenth century, and their legitimacy was debated once again a few decades later in the sixteenth century. This time, there were active waqfs, and their operations were affected by the state interventions due to the course of the debates (Mandaville 1979; Dumlu 2015). Besides, although the cash waqfs were initially supposed to use the capital in supporting the entrepreneurs via investing in their activities as in mudarabah and utilize the income for charity purposes, in time, they transformed into creditors that lend at interest by using prohibition-evading instruments (Okur 2005). The existence of interest-free loans given by the cash waqfs was also reported, but these were not common (Dumlu 2015).

Table 6.6 The alternative instruments to interest in Abrahamic religions

Instrument	*Islam*	*Christianity*	*Judaism*
Difference between spot and forward prices	•	•	•
Partnership with insurance		•	•
Pawnbroking	•	•	•
Penalty for late payment		•	•
Sale with a promise to repurchase	•	•	
Sale-leaseback	•	•	•

Source Calder (2016)

6.4.6 *Instruments in Christianity and Judaism*

It is not surprising that the cannon evading instruments did not pertain to the prohibition of interest in Islam. In medieval Europe, for example, many methods were developed to overcome the ban in Judaism (Cornell 2006) and Christianity (Koyama 2010). As Calder (2016) listed, the instruments used in Judaism and Christianity were highly similar to the ones used in Islam (Table 6.6).

In Christianity, *commenda*, a type of partnership (Koyama 2010), was almost the same as the mudaraba in Islam. Another instrument, *contractum trinius*, was formed of three contracts, one for investment, one for profit sale, and one for insurance. In brief, the lender was investing and paying an amount equal to a loan to the borrower. The borrower was insuring the investment against any loss. The lender was selling his rights on the profit of investment to the borrower. The sale price was a fixed percentage of investment, which was guaranteeing an income of interest (Henning 2007). By a *discretionary deposit*, a lender who deposited to a banker did not receive any interest. Instead, the banker gave a gift to the depositor at a value that was equal to an agreed rate of the amount that deposited capital (Koyama 2010).

In Judaism, *iska* was the same as the contractum trinius in Christianity. Besides, the difference between the spot and forward prices of goods was utilized in lending just the same as it is practiced in Islam (Cornell 2006).

Appendix 6.1: A Chronological Bibliography of Islamic Economics on Interest

Ahmad, S.M. 1946. *Economics of Islam: A Comparative Study*. Lahore: Sh.M.Ashraf.

Qureshi, Iqbal. 1946. *Islam and the Theory of Interest*. Lahore: Sh. M. Ashraf.

Abu Saud, M. 1957. "Islamic View of Riba and Interest." *Islamic Review* 45 (2): 9–16.

Rahman, Fazlur. 1958. "A Study of Commercial Interest in Islam." *Islamic Thought* 5 (4): 24–46.

Ahmed, I. 1963. "Islamic Economy and the Elimination of Interest." *Voice of Islam* 12 (2): 78–85.

Farid, Q. M. 1964. "Is Interest Obsolete?" *Voice of Islam* 13 (10): 495–502.

Rahman, Fazlur. 1964. "Riba and Interest." *Islamic Studies* 3 (1): 1–43.

Hamidullah, Muhammad. 1966. "A Suggestion for an Interest Free Islamic Monetary Fund." *Islamic Review* 43 (6): 11–12.

Zaman, S. H. 1966. "Islam Vis-a-Vis Interest Rate." *Islamic Culture* 40: 1–12.

Ahmad, Mahmud. 1967. "Semantics of the Theory of Interest." *Islamic Studies* 6 (2): 171–96.

Sheikh, N.A. 1967. "Modern Authorities on Economics Vindicate Islam's Interestless (Usuryless) Economic System—A Reply to Professor Sabri Ulgener 'Monetary Conditions of Economic Growth and the Islamic Concept of Interest.'" *The Islamic Review* 55: 11–13.

Ulgener, Sabri Fehmi. 1967. "Monetary Conditions of the Economic Growth and the Islamic Concept of Interest." *Islamic Review* 55 (2): 11–14.

Abbasi, Masud Ahmed. 1969. "Interest—An Economic Study on the Three Economic Systems." *Islamic Review* 57 (3–4): 28–32.

Ahmad, S.M. 1969. "Interest and Unemployment." *Islamic Studies* 8 (1): 9–46.

Mannan, Muhammad Abdul. 1970. "Islamic Theory of Capital and Interest." *Islamic Literature* 16 (4): 23–34.

Ghanameh, Abdul Hadi. 1976. "The Interestless Economy." In *Contemporary Aspects of Economic and Social Thinking in Islam*, 61–71. Muslim Student Association of US and Canada.

Uzair, Muḥammad. 1976. "Some Conceptual and Practical Aspects of Interest-Free Banking." *Islamic Studies* 15 (4): 247–69.

Ahmad, Ziauddin. 1978. "The Theory of Ribā." *Islamic Studies* 17 (4): 171–85.

Choudhury, Masudul Alam. 1979. "The Doctrine of Riba." *Journal of Development Studies, University of Peshawar* 2 (1).

Mandaville, Jon E. 1979. "Usurious Piety: The Cash Waqf Controversy in the Ottoman Empire." *International Journal of Middle East Studies* 10 (3): 289–308.

Abu Saud, M. 1980. "Money, Interest and Qirad." In *Studies in Islamic Economics*, edited by K. Ahmad, 59–84. Jeddah: International Centre for Research in Islamic Economics, King Abdulaziz University.

Hossain, K.T. 1980. "Running an Economy without Riba." In 152–56. Dhaka: Islamic Economic Research Bureau.

Sahid, M.A. 1980. "Interest in Islam Vis-a-Vis Modern Economy." *Pakistan Economist* 20 (33): 23–27.

Siddiqi, M. A. M. 1980. "Riba-Usury and Interest: Quran's Verdict Is Clear." *Islamic Order* 5: 25–42.

Uzair, H. 1980. "An Outline of Interest-Free Economy." In *Economic System of Islam*, 172–97. Karachi: National Bank of Pakistan.

Ahmed, Z. 1982. *Prohibition of Interest in Islam: Its Economic Implications and Modes of Interest-Free Banking and Finance*. Islamabad: The Third Pak-French Colloquium.

Ariff, Mohamed. 1982. "Monetary Policy in an Interest-Free Islamic Economy–Nature and Scope." In *Monetary and Fiscal Economics of Islam*, edited by Mohamed Ariff, 287–302. Jeddah: International Center for Research in Islamic Economics, King Abdulaziz University.

Choudhury, Masudul Alam. 1982. "Interest Rate and Intertemporal Efficiency in an Islamic Economy: Issue Revisited." *International Centre for Research in Islamic Economics, King Abdulaziz, Discussion Paper No:6.*

Haque, Ziaul. 1982. "The Nature of Riba Al-Nasi'a and Riba al-Fadl." *Islamic Studies* 21 (4): 19–38.

Karsten, I. 1982. "Efforts to Develop Islamic Financial Systems: Focus on the Abolition of the Fixed Interest Rate." *IMF Survey* 2 (4): 55–57.

Latif, M. Abdul. 1982. "Profit and Interest Compared." *Thoughts on Islamic Banking* 18: 109–12.

Mannan, Muhammad Abdul. 1982. "Allocative Efficiency, Decision and Welfare Criteria in an Interest-Free Islamic Economy: A Comparative Policy Approach." In *Monetary and Fiscal Economics of Islam*, edited by Mohamed Ariff, 43–74. Jeddah: International Center for Research in Islamic Economics, King Abdulaziz University.

Naqvi, Syed Nawab Haider. 1982a. "Interest Rate and Inter-Temporal Efficiency in an Islamic Economy." In *Monetary and Fiscal Economics of Islam*, edited by Mohamed Ariff, 75–100. Jeddah: International Center for Research in Islamic Economics, King Abdulaziz University.

Naqvi, Syed Nawab Haider. 1982b. *On Replacing the Institution of Interest in a Dynamic Islamic Economy*. Islamabad: Pakistan Institute of Development Economics.

Siddiqi, Muhammad N. 1982. "Islamic Laws on Riba and Their Economic Implication." *International Journal of Middle East Studies* 14 (11): 3–16.

Zarqa, Muhammad Anas. 1982. "Capital Allocation, Efficiency and Growth in an Interest-Free Islamic Economy." *Journal of Economics and Administration, King Abdulaziz University* 16: 43–55.

Haque, Ziaul. 1983. "Some Forms of Riba Al-Fadl in Trade and Commerce." *Islamic Studies* 22 (4): 73–95.

Zarqa, Muhammad Anas. 1982. 1983. "An Islamic Perspective on the Economics of Discounting in Project Evaluation." In *Fiscal Policy and Resource Allocation in Islam*, edited by Ziauddin Ahmed, Munawar Iqbal, and M. Fahim Khan, 179–223. Jeddah: International Centre for Research in Islamic Economics, King Abdulaziz University.

Chapra, M. Umer. 1984. "The Prohibition of Riba in Islam: An Evaluation of Some Objections." *American Journal of Islamic Social Sciences* 1 (2): 23.

Khan, Abdul Jabbar. 1984. "Elimination of Riba from the Banking System." *Journal of Islamic Banking and Finance* 1 (3): 24–44.

Chishti, Salim. 1985. "Relative Stability of Interest-Free Economy." *Journal of King Abdulaziz University: Islamic Economics* 3 (1): 3–12.

Hasan, Zubair. 1985. "Determination of Profit and Loss Sharing Ratios in Interest-Free Business Finance." *Journal of King Abdulaziz University: Islamic Economics* 3 (1).

Khan, Waqar Masood. 1985. *Towards an Interest-Free Islamic Economic System : A Theoretical Analysis of Prohibiting Debt Financing*. Leicester: Islamic Foundation.

Abu Saud, M. 1986. *Contemporary Economic Issues: Usury and Interest*. Zakat & Research Foundation.

Alkaff, Syed Hamed Abdul Rehman. 1986. *Does Islam Assign Any Value/Weight to Time Factor in Economic and Financial Transactions?* Karachi: Islamic Research Academy.

Khan, Mohsin S. 1986. "Islamic Interest-Free Banking: A Theoretical Analysis." *IMF Staff Papers* 33 (1): 1–27.

Naqvi, Syed Nawab Haider, and Asghar Qadir. 1986. *A Model of a Dynamic Islamic Economy and the Institution of Interest*. Essays in Islamic Economic Philosopy 4. Islamabad: Pakistan Institute of Development Economics.

Anwar, Muhammad. 1987. *Modeling Interest-Free Economy: A Study in Macroeconomics and Development*. International Institute of Islamic Thought (IIIT).

Uludağ, Süleyman. 1988. *İslamda Faiz Meselesine Yeni Bir Bakış* [A New View on the Issue of Interest in Islam]. İstanbul: Dergah Yayınları.

Haque, Ziaul. 1989. "Riba and Interest." *Journal of Islamic Banking and Finance* 6 (4): 7–9.

Khan, Waqar Masood. 1989. "Towards an Interest-Free Islamic Economic System." *Journal of King Abdulaziz University: Islamic Economics* 1: 33–38.

Mika'ilu, A. S. 1989. "On the Prohibition of Riba (Interest) and Its Implications for Optimum Economic Performance." *Hamdard Islamicus* 12 (1): 57–64.

Rosly, Saiful Azhar. 1989. "Welfare Implication of Interest-Free Bank Asset Management." *International Journal of Economics, Management and Accounting* 2 (2).

Ahmad, Ehsan. 1990. "Modelling Interest-Free Economy." *American Journal of Islamic Social Sciences* 7 (1): 111.

Metwally, Mukhtar M. 1990. "Towards Abolishing the Rate of Interest in Contemporary Islamic Societies." *Journal of King Abdulaziz University: Islamic Economics* 2 (1): 3–23.

Zaidi, N.A. 1990. "Riba: Its Economic Implications." *Journal of Islamic Banking and Finance* 7 (2): 7–14.

Ahmad, Z. 1991. "Thoughts on Riba and Interest." *Journal of Islamic Banking and Finance* 8 (2).

Haque, Ziaul. 1991. *Islam and Feudalism: The Economics of Riba, Interest and Profit*. Gulshan Publishers.

Ishfaq, M. 1991. "Anatomy of Riba and Interest." *Journal of Islamic Banking and Finance* 8 (3): 58–64.

Khan, M. Fahim. 1991. "Time Value of Money and Discounting in Islamic Perspective." *Review of Islamic Economics* 1 (2): 35–45.

Al-Saud, Mahmud Abu. 1992. *Islamic View of Riba (Usury and Interest)*. Quill Publishers.

Choudhury, Masudul Alam, and Uzir Abdul Malik. 1992. *The Foundations of Islamic Political Economy*. London: Palgrave Macmillan. https://public.ebookcentral.proquest.com/choice/publicfullrecord.aspx?p=5652786.

Mirakhor, Abbas. 1992. "Saving Behaviour in an Economy of Fixed Interest." *Islamic Economics* 4: 45–62.

Darrat, Ali F. 1993. "Comment's on Metwally's 'Towards Abolishing the Rate of Interest in Contemporary Islamic Societies.'" *Journal of King Abdulaziz University: Islamic Economics* 5: 39–49.

Mirakhor, Abbas. 1993. "Equilibrium in a Non-Interest Open Economy." *Journal of King Abdulaziz University: Islamic Economics* 5 (1): 3–23.

Zaman, Arshad. 1993. "Conceptual Foundation of Riba in Quran Hadith and Fiqh." *Journal of Islamic Banking and Finance, Karachi* 11 (1): 7–15.

Zangeneh, Hamid, and Ahmad Salam. 1993. "Central Banking in an Interest-Free Banking System." *Journal of King Abdulaziz University: Islamic Economics* 5: 25–36.

Ahmad, K. 1994. *Elimination of RIBA from the Economy: Concept and Problems*. Islamabad: Institute of Policy Studies.

Kahf, Monzer. 1994. "Time Value of Money and Discounting in Islamic Perspective: Re-Visited." *Review of Islamic Economics* 3 (2): 31–38.

Qadeeruddin, Ahmed. 1995. "What Is Riba?" *Journal of Islamic Banking and Finance* 12 (1): 7–49.

Saeed, Abdullah. 1995. "The Moral Context of the Prohibition of Ribā in Islam-Revisited." *The American Journal of Islamic Social Sciences* 12 (4): 496–517.

Shajari, H., and M. Kamalzadeh. 1995. "The Interest Rate and Islamic Banking." *Islamic Economic Studies* 3 (1).

Ahmad, Imad-ad-Dean. 1996. "Riba and Interest: Definitions and Implications." *Minaret of Freedom Institute Preprint Series*, 96.

Darrat, Ali F., and Shahid M. Ebrahim. 1996. "On the Design of Interest-Free Instruments." *Journal of King Abdulaziz University: Islamic Economics* 8 (1): 51–60.

Khan, M. Fahim. 1996. "A Simple Model of Income Determination, Growth and Economic Development in the Perspective of an Interest-Free Economy." In *Seminar Proceeding of Financing Development in Islam*, 79–108. Jeddah: Islamic Research and Training Institute.

Saeed, A. 1996. *Islamic Banking and Interest: A Study of Prohibition of Interest and Its Contemporary Interpretation*. Brill.

Siddiqui, Shamim Ahmad. 1996. "Factors of Production and Factor Returns Under Political Economy of Islam." *Journal of King AbdulAziz University: Islamic Economics* 8 (1): 3–28.

Bashar, Muhammad Lawal Ahmad. 1997. "Price Control in an Islamic Economy." *Journal of King Abdulaziz University: Islamic Economics* 9: 29–52.

Martin, Josh. 1997. "Islamic Banking Raises Interest." *Management Review* 86 (10): 25.

Billah, Mohd Masum. 2000. "Insurable Interest: Can the Modern Law Be Adopted in Takaful Operations?" *Arab Law Quarterly* 15 (2): 206–9.

Chapra, Umer. 2000. "Why Has Islam Prohibited Interest? Rationale behind the Prohibition of Interest." *Review of Islamic Economics* 9: 5–20.

Darrat, Ali F., and Abdel-Hameed M. Bashir. 2000. "Modeling Monetary Control in an Interest-Free Economy." *Islamic Economics* 12 (1): 13–19.

El-Gamal, Mahmoud A. 2000. "An Economic Explication of the Prohibition of Riba in Classical Islamic Jurisprudence." In *Proceedings of the Third Harvard University Forum on Islamic Finance*, 31–44. Cambridge: Center for Middle Eastern Studies, Harvard University.

Sharawy, Hesham M. 2000. "Understanding the Islamic Prohibition of Interest: A Guide to Aid Economic Cooperation between the Islamic and Western Worlds." *Georgia Journal of International and Comparative Law* 29 (1): 153–79.

Uthman, Usamah A. 2001. "Money, Interest and an Alternative Macroeconomic System." *International Journal of Economics, Management and Accounting* 9 (1): 101–14.

Ahmad, Abdel Rahman Yousri. 2002. "Prohibition of Riba in Islam: Its Economic Rationale and Implications." *Journal of Islamic Banking and Finance* 19 (2).

Bawany, Zakaria A. 2002. "Interest and Loan Free International Trade Import & Exports through RMU." In *The Proceeding of the 2002 International Conference on Stable and Just Global Monetary System, Kuala Lumpur*, 229–33.

Ahmad, Ausaf. 2003. "Islamic Banking in the Informal Sector: Interest-Free Solutions in Non-Muslim Societies." *Review of Islamic Economics* 14: 67–93.

El-Gamal, Mahmoud A. 2003. "Interest and the Paradox of Contemporary Islamic Law and Finance." *Fordham International Law Journal* 27 (1): 108–49.

Zarqa, Muhammad Anas. 1982. 2003. "Islamization of Economics: The Concept and Methodology." *Journal of King Abdulaziz University: Islamic Economics* 16 (1): 3–42.

Al-Masri, Rafic Yunus. 2004. "Are All Forms of Interest Prohibited?" *Journal of King Abdulaziz University: Islamic Economics* 17 (1): 37–41.

Bellalah, Mondher, and Siwar Ellouz. 2004. "Islamic Finance, Interest Rates and Islamic Banking—A Survey of the Literature." *Finance India* 18: 533–46.

Gafoor, A.L.M. Abdul. 2004. *Interest, Usury, Riba and the Operational Costs of a Bank.* Kuala Lumpur: AS Noordeen.

Samad, Abdus. 2004. "Performance of Interest-Free Islamic Banks Vis-à-Vis Interest-Based Conventional Banks of Bahrain." *International Journal of Economics, Management and Accounting* 12 (2): 1–14.

Shams, Rasul. 2004. "A Critical Assessment of Islamic Economics." Discussion Paper 281. Hamburg Institute of International Economics.

Siddiqi, Muhammad Nejatullah. 2004. *Riba, Bank Interest and the Rationale of Its Prohibition.* Jeddah: Islamic Research and Training Institute.

Afzal, Mohammad. 2005. "Debate over Interest: Islamic Perspective." *Journal of Economic & Social Research* 7 (1): 51–69.

Dadgar, Y. 2005. *Analysis of Relationship Between Interest Free Financial System and Sustainable Development*. London: Palgrave.

Khan, M. Fahim, and Abdulkader Thomas. 2005. "The Challenge in Pakistan." In *Interest in Islamic Economics: Understanding Riba*, edited by Abdulkader Thomas, 134–37. New York: Routledge.

Khan, Waqar Masood. 2005. *Transition to a Riba-Free Economy*. New Delhi: Adam Publishers.

Siddiqui, Shamim Ahmad. 2005. "Understanding and Eliminating Riba: Can Islamic Financial Instruments Be Meaningfully Implemented?" *Journal of Management and Social Sciences* 1 (2): 187–203.

Thomas, Abdulkader. 2005. "What Is Riba?" In *Interest in Islamic Economics: Understanding Riba*, edited by Abdulkader Thomas, 124–33. New York: Routledge.

Ahmad, Abu Umar Faruq, and M Kabir Hassan. 2006. "The Time Value of Money Concept in Islamic Finance." *American Journal of Islamic Social Sciences* 23 (1): 66.

Chapra, Muhammad Umer. 2006. "The Nature of Riba in Islam." *Journal of Islamic Economics, Banking and Finance* 2 (1): 7–25.

DeLorenzo, Yusuf Talal. 2006. "Introduction to Understanding Riba." In *Interest in Islamic Economics: Understanding Riba*, edited by Abdulkadir Thomas, 1–9. New York: Routledge.

Deniz, Abdülbaki. 2006. "İslam Hukukunda Illet Kavramı ve Faizin Illeti [Cause in Islamic Law and Cause of Interest]." Master Thesis, İstanbul: Uludağ University.

El-Gamal, Mahmoud A. 2006. "An Attempt to Understand the Economic Wisdom (Hikma) in the Prohibition of Riba." In *Interest in Islamic Economics Understanding Riba*, edited by Abdulkadir Thomas, 111–23. New York: Routledge.

Iqbal, Muhammad Mazhar. 2006. "A Broader Definition of Riba." *Pakistan Institute of Development Economics Working Paper*.

Kahf, Monzer. 2006. "Maqasid al Shari'ah in the Prohibition of Riba and Their Implications for Modern Islamic Finance." In *IIUM International Conference on Maqasid Al-Shari'ah*.

Khalil, Emad H. 2006. "An Overview of the Shari'a Prohibition of Riba." In *Interest in Islamic Economics: Understanding Riba*, edited by Abdulkadir Thomas, 53–67. New York: Routledge.

Khalil, Emad H, and Abdulkadir Thomas. 2006. "The Modern Debate over Riba in Egypt." In *Interest in Islamic Economics: Understanding Riba*, edited by Abdulkadir Thomas, 68–94. New York: Routledge.

Khan, Mohammad Mansoor, and M. Ishaq Bhatti. 2006. "Why Interest-Free Banking and Finance Movement Failed in Pakistan." *Humanomics* 22 (3): 145–61.

Siddiqui, Shamim Ahmad. 2006. "The Controversy over Time Value of Money among Contemporary Muslim Economists." *Journal of Management and Social Sciences* 2 (2): 144–53.

Ahmad, Shafa'at. 2007. "Riba in Pre-Islamic Arabia." In *Riba, Modern and Islamic Banking: A Critique*, edited by Nafis Ahmad Siddiqui, Mohd. Zahir, and Abu Nazim, 20–28. Indset Monograph Series on Islam and Qur'an. Hyderabad: Indian School of Excellence Trust.

Ali, A.H. 2007. "Riba and the Credit Needs of the Muslims." In *Riba, Modern and Islamic Banking: A Critique*, edited by Nafis Ahmad Siddiqui, Mohd. Zahir, and Abu Nazim, 181–239. Hyderabad: Indian School of Excellence Trust.

Aziz, Farooq. 2007. "Qur'anic Concept of Riba (Interest)." *IBT Journal of Business Studies* 3 (2).

Chapra, M. Umer. 2007. "The Case against Interest: Is It Compelling?" *Thunderbird International Business Review* 49 (2): 161–86.

Farooq, Mohammad. 2007. "The Riba-Interest Equivalence: Is There an Ijma (Consensus)?" *Transnational Dispute Management* 4 (5).

Nyazee, Imran Ahsan. 2007. "The Rules and Definition of Riba." In *Riba, Modern and Islamic Banking: A Critique*, edited by Nafis Ahmad Siddiqui, Mohd. Zahir, and Abu Nazim, 153–79. Indset Monograph Series on Islam and Qur'an. Hyderabad: Indian School of Excellence Trust.

Aziz, Farooq, Muhammad Mahmud, and Emadul Karim. 2008. "An Analytical Review of Different Concepts of Riba (Interest) in the Sub-Continent." *KASBIT Business Journal* 1 (1): 36–43.

Kula, Erhun. 2008. "Is Contemporary Interest Rate in Conflict with Islamic Ethics?" *Kyklos* 61 (1): 45–64.

Mussavian, Sayed Abbas. 2008. "The Theories of Riba and Interest." *Eghtesad-e Islami* 7 (27): 67–100.

Batcha, Azah Atikah Binti Anwar. 2009. *Time Value of Money and Riba: Islamic Perspective*. Kuala Lumpur: INCEIF.

Borhan. 2009. "Rationale and Consequences of the Prohibition of Riba in an Islamic Economic System." *Innovatio* 8 (2): 291–312.

Farooq, Mohammad. 2009a. "Riba, Interest and Six Hadiths: Do We Have a Definition or a Conundrum?" *Review of Islamic Economics* 13 (1): 105–41.

Farooq, Mohammad. 2009b. "The Riba-Interest Equation and Islam: Reexamination of the Traditional Arguments." *Global Journal of Finance and Economics* 6 (2): 99–111.

Zakir Hossain, Mohammad. 2009. "Why Is Interest Prohibited in Islam? A Statistical Justification." *Humanomics* 25 (4): 241–53.

Azhar, Rauf. 2010. *Economics of an Islamic Economy*. Leiden: Brill.

Iqbal, Muhammad Mazhar. 2010. "Prohibition of Interest and Economic Rationality." *Arab Law Quarterly* 24 (3): 293–308.

Sugema, Iman, Toni Bakhtiar, and Jaenal Effendi. 2010. "Interest versus Profit-Loss Sharing Credit Contract: Efficiency and Welfare Implications." *International Research Journal of Finance and Economics* 45 (1): 58–67.

Ahmad, Ashfaq, Kashih-ur Rehman, and Asad Afzal Humayoun. 2011. "Islamic Banking and Prohibition of Riba/Interest." *African Journal of Business Management* 5 (5): 1763–67.

Balala, Maha-Hanaan. 2011. *Islamic Finance and Law: Theory and Practice in a Globalized World*. International Library of Economics 5. London: I.B. Tauris.

El Diwany, Tarek. 2011. *Faiz Sorunu [The Problem with Interest]*. İstanbul: İz Yayıncılık.

Iqbal, Zamir, and Abbas Mirakhor. 2011. *An Introduction to Islamic Finance: Theory and Practice*. John Wiley & Sons.

Salleh, Murizah Osman, Aziz Jaafar, and Muhammed Shahid Ebrahim. 2011. "The Inhibition of Usury (Riba an-Nasi'ah) and the Economic Underdevelopment of the Muslim World." *Available at SSRN 1941409*. https://ssrn.com/abstract=1941409.

Farooq, Mohammad. 2012a. "Exploitation, Profit and the Riba-interest Reductionism." *International Journal of Islamic and Middle Eastern Finance and Management* 5 (4): 292–320.

Farooq, Muhammad. 2012b. "Interest, Usury and Its Impact on the Economy." *Dialogue* 7 (3): 265–76.

Nurrachmi, Rininta, Mia Fathia, Ashanee Mad-ahdin, Ninasrin Raden-armad, and Rulia Akhtar. 2012. "Time Value of Money in Islamic Perspective and the Practice in Islamic Banking Implications." *Available at MPRA No: 46818*. https://mpra.ub.uni-muenchen.de/46818/.

Swartz, Nico P. 2012. "The Prevention of Over-Indebtedness: The Problem of Interest and the Islamic Response." *African Journal of Business Management* 6 (37). Academic Journals: 10099–108.

Abdul Khir, Mohamed Fairooz. 2013. "The Concept of the Time Value of Money: A Shari'ah Viewpoint." *International Journal of Excellence in Islamic Banking and Finance* 3 (2): 1–15.

Khan, Muhammad Akram. 2013. *What Is Wrong with Islamic Economics? Analysing the Present State and Future Agenda*. UK: Edward Elgar.

Kahf, Monzer. 2014. "Riba in Islamic Economics and Finance." In *Handbook on Islam and Economic Life*, edited by M. Kabir Hassan and Mervyn K. Lewis, 132–52. Edward Elgar Publishing.

Razi, Naseem. 2014. "Socio-Ethical Dimensions of Islamic Economy and Issue of Modern Interest and (Riba): An Analysis in the Light of the Economy of the Muslim World." *Journal of Islamic Banking and Finance* 2 (2): 27–42.

Siddiqui, Shamim A. 2014. "Riba, Time Value of Money and Discounting." In *Handbook on Islam and Economic Life*, edited by M. Kabir Hassan and Mervyn K. Lewis, 113–31. Edward Elgar Publishing.

Askari, Hossein, Zamir Iqbal, and Abbas Mirakhor. 2015. *Introduction to Islamic Economics: Theory and Application*. Singapore: John Wiley & Sons.

Chapra, Muhammad Umer. 2015. *Prohibition of Interest: Does It Make Sense*. Durban: Islamic Dawah Movement.

Kamla, Rania, and Rana Alsoufi. 2015. "Critical Muslim Intellectuals' Discourse and the Issue of 'Interest'(Ribā): Implications for Islamic Accounting and Banking." *Accounting Forum* 39 (2): 140–54.

Siddique, Muhammad Abubakar, and Memoona Rahim. 2015. "The Concepts of Discounting and Time Value of Money in Islamic Capital Budgeting Framework: A Theoretical Study." *Journal of Islamic Banking and Finance* 32 (1): 23–29.

Sofhian, Sultan Amai Gorontalo. 2015. "The Rationality Prohibition of Riba (Usury)." *Al-Ulum* 15 (1): 237–66.

Suharto, Ugi. 2015. "Islamic Finance as an Interest Free Finance: A Confusing Terminology." In *International Congress on Islamic Economics and Finance*. Sakarya.

Abbasi, M.A. 2016. *Bank Interest and Islam*. Islamabad: Emel Publication.

Bilal, Muhammad Talha, Hafiz Muhammad Tayyab, Muhammad Arshad Ullah, and Arshad Mahmood. 2016. "Islam Prohibits Interest." *International Journal of Humanities and Social Science* 1 (5): 1–11.

Calder, Ryan. 2016. "God's Technicians: Religious Jurists and the Usury Ban in Judaism, Christianity, and Islam." *European Journal of Sociology* 57 (2): 207–57.

Shahar, Wan Shahzlinda Shah Wan, Ummi Munirah Syuhada Mohamad Zan, and Wan Suraya Wan Hassin. 2016. "The Implication of Usury (Riba) in Economic: A Critique." In *Proceeding of the 3rd International Conference on Management & Muamalah 2016*.

Farooq, Mohammad. 2017. "Toward Defining and Understanding Riba: An Outline Essay." *Available at SSRN 1723803*.

Gul, Ali Riza. 2017. "The Concept of Jahiliyya Usury (Riba) as the Basis of Interest Prohibition in Islam." *Cumhuriyet Theology Journal* 21 (1): 701–48.

Ahmad, Salman, Muhammad Amjad, and Ejaz Aslam. 2018. "Types of Interest in Islamic Law Analysis and Application." *Pakistan Journal of Islamic Research* 18 (2).

Choudhury, Masudul Alam, Asmak AB Rahman, and Abul Hasan. 2018. "Trade versus Riba in the Qur'ān with a Critique of the Role of

Bank-Saving." *International Journal of Law and Management* 60 (2): 701–16.

Erdem, Ekrem. 2018. "Kur'an'da Riba (Faiz) Ayetlerinin Kademeli Nüzulü ve Üslubu: İslam'ın Ticaret, Infak ve Finans Sistemi Üzerinden Bir Inceleme [The Gradual Revelation and Style of the Riba (Interest) Verses in Quran: An Enquiry Regarding the Trade, Aid and Finance System of Islam]." In *İslam Iktisadı Perspektifinden Faiz [Interest from the Perspective of Islamic Economics]*, edited by Taha Eğri and Zeynep Hafsa Orhan, 1–51. İstanbul: İktisat Yayınları.

Rashidian, Somaye, Amrollah Amini, and Ali Masuminia. 2018. "Criticizing Subjective Origins of Interest Rate, a Rational Approach Based on Islamic Philosophy." *Tahghighat-e-Eghtesadi* 53 (3): 597–617.

Suharto, Ugi. 2018. "Riba and Interest in Islamic Finance: Semantic and Terminological Issue." *International Journal of Islamic and Middle Eastern Finance and Management* 11 (1): 131–38.

Aji, Hendy Mustiko, Izra Berakon, and Muamar Nur Kholid. 2019. "The Moderating Role of Knowledge about Riba on Intention to Use E-Money: Findings from Indonesia." In *2019 IEEE 6th International Conference on Industrial Engineering and Applications (ICIEA)*, 588–93.

Al Hasani, Mohammed. 2019. "Analysis of the Types of Interest riba in Islamic Law." *Journal of Islamic Banking & Finance* 36 (4).

Borroni, Andrea. 2019. "A Comparative Survey on Islamic Riba and Western Usury." *Stato, Chiese e Pluralismo Confessionale* 4.

El-Gamal, Mahmoud. 2019. "Al-Sanhuri on Riba (Translation of Excerpt from Abdul-Razzaq al-Sanhuri's Sources of Rights in Islamic Jurisprudence)." Available at SSRN 3511691.

Farooq, Mohammad. 2019a. "Banking Structure and Riba-Interest Equation: The Case for Ta'awuni (Cooperative) Finance." *Journal of Islamic Finance Studies* 5 (2): 90–108.

Farooq, Mohammad. 2019b. "Rent-Seeking Behaviour and Ẓulm (Injustice/Exploitation) beyond Ribā-Interest Equation." *ISRA International Journal of Islamic Finance.*

Fasa, Muhammad Iqbal, Itsla Yunisva Aviva, Yayan Firmansah, and Suharto Suharto. 2019. "Controversy on Riba Prohibition: Maqashid Shariah Perspective." *International Journal of Islamic Economics* 1 (2): 124–35.

Fontaine, Rodrigue. 2019. "Perception of Riba among the Muslims in Malaysia: An Exploratory Study." *Journal of Islamic Finance* 8 (1): 36–47.

Iqbal, Muhammad Mazhar, and Anwar Shah. 2019. "Economic Rationale of the Prohibition of Interest: A New Aspect." *Islamic Studies* 58 (4): 503–17.

Kusmiati, Mia. 2019. "Home Ownership Loans through Economy Shariah to Avoid Riba." In *Proceedings International Conference on Social Science-ICOSS*. Vol. 1.

Mehfooz, Musferah. 2019. "Provision of Riba by Religious Faith." In *The Growth of Islamic Finance and Banking: Innovation, Governance and Risk Mitigation*, edited by Hussain Mohi-ud-Din Qadri and M. Ishaq Bhatti, 152–66. Routledge.

Nawaz, Mohammad. 2019. "Analysis of Interest riba in Islamic Law: Definition of Interest and Its Characteristics." *Journal of Islamic Banking & Finance* 36 (2).

Ramli, Yanto, Eko Tama Putra Saratian, Mochamad Soelton, and Margono Setiawan. 2019. "Riba Prohibition for the Community Economic Sustainability." In *International Conference on Community Development*, 2:612–15.

Siddique, Muhammad Zahid, and Muhammad Mushtaq Ahmad. 2019. "Demystifying Riba through the Methodology of Muslim Jurists." *Islamic Studies* 58 (2): 169.

Suman, Agus, and Ahmad Imam Mawardi. 2019. "Riba in Cognitive Behavioral Theory." In *2018 International Conference on Islamic Economics and Business (ICONIES 2018)*. Atlantis Press.

Suzuki, Yasushi. 2019. "Riba, Usury and Keynes." *Islam and Civilisational Renewal ICR Journal* 10 (2): 175–88.

Yusof, Ahmad Yusri Aiman Mat. 2019. "The Concepts of Riba, Gharar and Maysir in Islamic Finance." In *Islamic Finance Mini Pupillage Programme Case Studies*, 5–16. Malaysian Institute of Accountants.

Ahroum, Rida, Othmane Touri, and Boujemâa Achchab. 2020. "Murabaha and Musharakah Moutanaquissah Pricing: An Interest-Free Approach." *Journal of Islamic Accounting and Business Research* 11 (1): 2012–2215.

Aji, Hendy Mustiko, Izra Berakon, and Alex Fahrur Riza. 2020. "The Effects of Subjective Norm and Knowledge about Riba on Intention to Use E-Money in Indonesia." *Journal of Islamic Marketing*.

Dayyan, Muhammad, and Rifyal Dahlawy Chalil. 2020. "The Attitude of Merchants towards Fatwa on Riba and Conventional Bank in Langsa." *Jurnal Ekonomi Dan Keuangan Islam* 9.

Gani, Ibrahim Musa. 2020. "Interest (Riba) and Its Consequence on the Economy." *Journal of Islamic, Social, Economics and Development* 5 (30): 13–22.

Idrees, Muhammad, and Hafiz Muhammad Sani. 2020. "Comparative Analysis between Conventional and Riba-Free Banking." *The International Research Journal Department of Usooluddin* 4 (1): 1–18.

Khan, Haseeb. 2020. "Riba in Islamic Banking and Its Contemporary Applications; in the Seerah of Muhammad (PBUH)." Available at SSRN 3527320.

Khan, Muhammad Akram. 2020. "Riba in Islamic Finance: Some Fresh Insights." *Journal of Economic and Social Thought* 7 (1): 25–40.

Mohsin, Magda Ismail Abdel. 2020. "A Fresh View on Zakah as a Socio-Financial Tool to Promote Ethics, Eliminate Riba and Reduce Poverty." *International Journal of Management and Applied Research* 7 (1): 55–71.

Nyazee, Imran Ahsan. 2020. "The Definition of Riba or the Failure of Modern Scholars to Understand the True Meaning of Riba." Available at SSRN 3522646.

Oktaviany, Suhannisah, Pepi Idayanti Marpaung, and Dewi Maharani Ginting. 2020. "Riba Free Financing Based on Rental Business." In *Proceeding International Seminar of Islamic Studies*, 1:83–90.

Suzuki, Yasushi, and Mohammad Dulal Miah. 2020. "Shari'ah-Compliant Benchmark and Shari'ah-Based 'Raf'al-Haraj' Benchmark on Prohibition of Riba." *International Journal of Islamic and Middle Eastern Finance and Management* ahead-of-print.

Appendix 6.2: The Translation of the Term *Riba* into English

See Table 6.7.

Table 6.7 The term Riba in the Quran's English translations

		Sure:Verse							
	Translation	*2:275-a*	*2:275-b*	*2:275-c*	*2:276*	*2:278*	*3:130*	*4:161*	*30:39*
1	Abdul Majid Daryabadi	usury	usury	usury	usury	usury	usury	usury	gift
2	Abdullah Yusuf Ali	usury	usury	usury	usury	usury	usury	usury	lay out
3	Ali Quli Qara	usury	usury	usury	usury	usury	usury	usury	usury
4	Amatul Rahman Omar	usury and interest	usury and interest	interest	usury and interest	usury and interest	usury and interest	interest and usury	interest and usury
5	Faridul Haque	usury	usury	usury	usury	usury	usury	usury	usury
6	Hajj Abdalhaq and Aisha Bewley	usury	usury	usury	usury	usury	usury	usury	usurious intent
7	Hamid S. Aziz	usury	usury	usury	usury	usury	usury	usury	usury
8	IFTA Committee	usury	usury	usury	usury	usury	usury	usury	usury
9	M. Hilali and Muhsin Khan	riba (usury)	riba (usury)	riba (usury)	riba (usury)	riba (usury)	riba (usury)	riba (usury)	gift
10	M. J. Ahmed and Samira [illegible]	growth/interest/usury	growth/ interest/ usury	growth/ interest/ usury	growth/ interest/ usury	growth /interest /usury	growth /increase /interest	interest /usury	growth /increase /interest
[illegible]	[illegible]	[illegible]	usury	usury	usury	usury	usurious interest	usury	usury

(continued)

Table 6.7 (continued)

		Sure:Verse							
	Translation	*2:275-a*	*2:275-b*	*2:275-c*	*2:276*	*2:278*	*3:130*	*4:161*	*30:39*
12	Muhammad Asad	usury	usury	usury	usurious gain	usury	usury	usury	usury
13	Muhammad Habib Shakir	usury	usury	usury	usury	usury	usury	usury	usury
14	Muhammad Mahmud Ghali	riba (interest or usury)	riba	riba	riba (interest or other unlawful)	riba	riba (usury, interest)	riba (usury and other unlawful)	riba (usury and other unlawful)
15	Muhammad Marmaduke Pickthall	usury	usury	usury	usury	usury	usury	usury	usury
16	Sheikh Muhammad Sarwar	interest	interest	interest	interest	interest	interest	usury	interest
17	Syed Vickar Ahamed	interest	usury	usury	usury	usury	usury	interest (usury)	interest
18	Thomas B. Irving	interest	interest	interest	usury	interest	usury	usury	usury
19	Wahiduddin Khan	usury	usury	usury	usury	usury	usury	usury	usury

References

Ahmad, Imad-ad-Dean. 1996. "Riba and Interest: Definitions and Implications." *Minaret of Freedom Institute Preprint Series*, 96.

Ahmad, Shafa'at. 2007. "Riba in Pre-Islamic Arabia." In *Riba, Modern and Islamic Banking: A Critique*, edited by Nafis Ahmad Siddiqui, Mohd. Zahir, and Abu Nazim, 20–28. Indset Monograph Series on Islam and Qur'an. Hyderabad: Indian School of Excellence Trust.

Ahmad, Ziauddin. 1978. "The Theory of Ribā." *Islamic Studies* 17 (4): 171–85.

Al-Masri, Rafic Yunus. 2004. "Are All Forms of Interest Prohibited?" *Journal of King Abdulaziz University: Islamic Economics* 17 (1): 37–41.

Arif, Muhammad. 1985. "Toward a Definition of Islamic Economics: Some Scientific Considerations." *Journal of King Abdulaziz University: Islamic Economics* 2 (2): 79–93.

Askari, Hossein, Zamir Iqbal, and Abbas Mirakhor. 2015. *Introduction to Islamic Economics: Theory and Application*. Singapore: Wiley.

Azhar, Rauf. 2019. *İslam Iktisadının Ekonomisi* [Economics of an Islamic Economy]. İstanbul: İktisat Yayınları.

Azid, Toseef. 2010. "Anthology of Islamic Economics: Review of Some Basic Issues." *Review of Islamic Economics* 13 (2): 165–94.

Aziz, Farooq, Muhammad Mahmud, and Emadul Karim. 2008. "An Analytical Review of Different Concepts of Riba (Interest) in the Sub-Continent." *KASBIT Business Journal* 1 (1): 36–43.

Balala, Maha-Hanaan. 2011. *Islamic Finance and Law: Theory and Practice in a Globalized World*. International Library of Economics 5. London: I.B. Tauris.

Bulut, Mehmet, and Cem Korkut. 2017. "A Look at Cash Waqfs as Islamic Financial Institutions and Instruments." In *Critical Issues and Challenges in Islamic Economics and Finance Development*, edited by Velid Efendic, Fikret Hadzic, and Hylmun Izhar, 85–96. Palgrave Macmillan.

Calder, Ryan. 2016. "God's Technicians: Religious Jurists and the Usury Ban in Judaism, Christianity, and Islam." *European Journal of Sociology* 57 (2): 207–57.

Chapra, Muhammad Umer. 1996. *What Is Islamic Economics?* Vol. 9. Islamic Development Bank, Islamic Research and Training Institute.

———. 2000. "Is It Necessary to Have Islamic Economics?" *The Journal of Socio-Economics* 29 (1): 21–37.

———. 2006. "The Nature of Riba in Islam." *Journal of Islamic Economics, Banking and Finance* 2 (1): 7–25.

Choudhury, Masudul Alam, and Uzir Abdul Malik. 1992. *The Foundations of Islamic Political Economy*. London: Palgrave Macmillan Limited. https://public.ebookcentral.proquest.com/choice/publicfullrecord.aspx?p=5652786.

Cohen, Suleiman Ibrahim. 2017. "Islamic Economics and Modern Economies: Resetting the Research Agenda." *Journal of Global Economics* 5 (2).

Cornell, Vincent J. 2006. "In the Shadow of Deuteronomy: Approaches to Interest and Usury in Judaism and Christianity." In *Interest in Islamic Economics: Understanding Riba*, edited by Abdulkadir Thomas, 13–24. New York: Routledge.

DeLorenzo, Yusuf Talal. 2006. "Introduction to Understanding Riba." In *Interest in Islamic Economics: Understanding Riba*, edited by Abdulkadir Thomas, 1–9. New York: Routledge.

Deniz, Abdülbaki. 2006. "İslam Hukukunda Illet Kavramı ve Faizin Illeti [Cause in Islamic Law and Cause of Interest]." Master Thesis, İstanbul: Uludağ University.

Dumlu, Emrullah. 2015. "XVI. Yüzyıl Osmanlı Uleması Arasında Para Vakıfları Etrafinda Cereyan Eden Tartışmalar (Ebussuûd, İbn Kemal-Çivizâde, Birgivî) [The Discussions among XVI. Century Ottoman Scholars about the Cash Waqfs (Ebussuud, İbn Kemal-Çivizade, Birgivi)]." *İlahiyat Tetkikleri Dergisi (İLTED)* 2 (44): 303–37.

Erdem, Ekrem. 2018. "Kur'an'da Riba (Faiz) Ayetlerinin Kademeli Nüzulü ve Üslubu: İslam'ın Ticaret, Infak ve Finans Sistemi Üzerinden Bir Inceleme [The Gradual Revelation and Style of the Riba (Interest) Verses in Quran: An Enquiry Regarding the Trade, Aid and Finance System of Islam]." In *İslam Iktisadı Perspektifinden Faiz* [Interest from the Perspective of Islamic Economics], edited by Taha Eğri and Zeynep Hafsa Orhan, 1–51. İstanbul: İktisat Yayınları.

Farooq, Mohammad. 2007. "The Riba-Interest Equivalence: Is There an Ijma (Consensus)?" *Transnational Dispute Management* 4 (5).

Ghazanfar, Shaikh M., and Abdul Azim Islahi. 2003. "Explorations in Medieval Arab-Islamic Economic Thought—Some Aspects of Ibn Taimiyah's Economics." In *Medieval Islamic Economic Thought—Filling the Great Gap in European Economics*, edited by Shaikh M. Ghazanfar, 53–71. Rouledge-Curzon.

Grassie, William. 2010. *The New Sciences of Religion: Exploring Spirituality from the Outside in and Bottom Up*. New York: Palgrave Macmillan.

Gül, Ali Rıza. 2017. "İslâm'daki Faiz Yasağının Temeli Olarak Câhiliye Ribâsı Kavramı [The Concept of Jahiliyya Usury (Riba) as the Basis of Interest Prohibition in Islam]." *Cumhuriyet Theology Journal* 21 (1): 701–48.

Hamidullah, Muhammed. 1980. *İslam Peygamberi* [The Prophet of Islam]. İstanbul: İrfan Yayınevi.

Haneef, Mohamed Aslam. 2005. "Can There Be an Economics Based on Religion? The Case of Islamic Economics." *Post-Autistic Economics Review* 34: 41–52.

Haneef, Mohamed Aslam, and Hafas Furqani. 2011. "Methodology of Islamic Economics: Overview of Present State and Future Direction." *International Journal of Economics, Management and Accounting* 19 (1): 1–26.

Hasan, Zubair. 2016. "Evolution of Islamic Economics: A Critical Analyses." *ISRA International Journal of Islamic Finance* 8 (2): 9–25.
Hasanuzzaman, S M. 1984. "Definition of Islamic Economics." *Journal of Research in Islamic Economics* 1 (2): 49–50.
Hasenat Quranic Research Application (version 6.1). 2015. Last updated on 11th May 2019.
Henning, Jozeph Johannes. 2007. "The Mediaeval Contractum Trinius and the Law of Partnership." *Fundamina: A Journal of Legal History* 13 (2): 33–49.
Kahf, Monzer. 2014. "Islamic Economics: Notes on Definition and Methodology." In *Islamic Economics—On Definition and Methodology*, edited by Sercan Karadoğan, 27–57. İstanbul: The Institute of Islamic Economics.
Kamla, Rania, and Rana Alsoufi. 2015. "Critical Muslim Intellectuals' Discourse and the Issue of 'Interest'(Ribā): Implications for Islamic Accounting and Banking." *Accounting Forum* 39 (2): 140–54.
Karayiannis, Anastassios D., and Aristides N. Hatzis. 2010. "Morality, Social Norms and the Rule of Law as Transaction Cost-Saving Devices: The Case of Ancient Athens." *European Journal of Law and Economics* 33 (3): 621–43.
Khalil, Emad H. 2006. "An Overview of the Shari'a Prohibition of Riba." In *Interest in Islamic Economics: Understanding Riba*, edited by Abdulkadir Thomas, 53–67. New York: Routledge.
Khalil, Emad H, and Abdulkadir Thomas. 2006. "The Modern Debate over Riba in Egypt." In *Interest in Islamic Economics: Understanding Riba*, edited by Abdulkadir Thomas, 68–94. New York: Routledge.
Khan, Muhammad Akram. 1984. "Islamic Economics: Nature and Need." *Journal of King Abdulaziz University: Islamic Economics* 1 (2): 51–55.
———. 1994. *An Introduction to Islamic Economics*. Islamabad: International Institute of Islamic Thought.
———. 2013. *What Is Wrong with Islamic Economics? Analysing the Present State and Future Agenda*. UK: Edward Elgar.
———. 2020. "Riba in Islamic Finance: Some Fresh Insights." *Journal of Economic and Social Thought* 7 (1): 25–40.
Koehler, Benedikt. 2014. *Early Islam and the Birth of Capitalism*. United States: Lexington Books.
Koyama, Mark. 2010. "Evading the Taint of Usury." *Explorations in Economic History* 47 (4).
Kuran, Timur, and Jared Rubin. 2017. "The Financial Power of the Powerless: Socio-economic Status and Interest Rates Under Partial Rule of Law." *The Economic Journal* 128 (609): 758–96.
Lawal, Ibrahim Mohammad. 2016. "Riba (Usury); A Tool That Should Be Carved Out of Financial Transactions." *Turkish Journal of Islamic Economics* 3 (2): 13–24.

Mandaville, Jon E. 1979. "Usurious Piety: The Cash Waqf Controversy in the Ottoman Empire." *International Journal of Middle East Studies* 10 (3): 289–308.

Mirakhor, Abbas, and Iqbal Zaidi. 2007. "Profit-and-Loss Sharing Contracts in Islamic Finance." In *Handbook of Islamic Banking*, edited by M. Kabir Hassan and Mervyn K. Lewis, 49–63. UK: Edward Elgar.

North, Douglass C. 1991. "Institutions." *Journal of Economic Perspectives* 5 (1): 97–112.

Okur, Kaşif Hamdi. 2005. "Para Vakıfları Bağlamında Osmanlı Hukuk Düzeni ve Ebussuud Efendinin Hukuk Anlayışı Üzerine Bazı Değerlendirmeler [Some Notes on Ottoman Law Order and Ebussuud Efendi's Juridical Views Concerning Cash Waqfs in Ottoman Empire]." *Hitit Üniversitesi İlahiyat Fakültesi Dergisi* 4 (7–8): 33–58.

Rahman, Fazlur. 1964. "Riba and Interest." *Islamic Studies* 3 (1): 1–43.

Schumpeter, Joseph A. 1986. *History of Economic Analysis*. Routledge.

Siddiqi, Muhammad Nejatullah. 1982. *Recent Works on History of Economic Thought in Islam: A Survey*. International Centre for Research in Islamic Economics, King Abdulaziz University.

———. 2004. *Riba, Bank Interest and the Rationale of Its Prohibition*. Jeddah: Islamic Research and Training Institute.

Suharto, Ugi. 2018. "Riba and Interest in Islamic Finance: Semantic and Terminological Issue." *International Journal of Islamic and Middle Eastern Finance and Management* 11 (1): 131–38.

Thomson Reuters. 2018. "Islamic Finance Development Report."

Uludağ, Süleyman. 1988. *İslamda Faiz Meselesine Yeni Bir Bakış [A New View on the Issue of Interest in Islam]*. İstanbul: Dergah Yayınları.

Zarqa, Muhammad Anas. 2003. "Islamization of Economics: The Concept and Methodology." *Journal of King Abdulaziz University: Islamic Economics* 16 (1): 3–42.

CHAPTER 7

Time Preference and Price Control in Islamic Economics

Most of the Muslim jurists decreed that interest is the same as riba, and it is banned following the mainstream view of Islamic economists. In consequence, the prohibition of interest became the most distinctive feature of Islamic economics that did not exist within the conventional systems.

However, some economists claimed that time preference is an inevitable cause of interest, and banning interest or limiting its rate has non-negligible destructive implications on the market. Islamic economists' plausible interpretations of these two issues would help in the further success of the Islamic economic system and the interest-free financial instruments. They may either refute or entirely or partially acknowledge the assertions on time preference and interest rate control. Whatever their conclusion is, insofar as it is plausible, their arguments on the interest-free system would be convincing for others.

In the first section of the chapter, beginning from the middle of the twentieth century, the interpretation of Islamic economists on the concepts of the time value of money and time preference is reviewed in detail. Their approach to Böhm-Bawerk's theory is particularly overviewed.

In the second section, the Islamic economists' consideration of the consequences of interest rate control within the frame of price control phenomena is reviewed.

C. Eyerci, *The Causes and Consequences of Interest Theory*,
https://doi.org/10.1007/978-3-030-78702-8_7

7.1 Time Preference in Islamic Economics Literature

The concept of *time* in Islamic economics has been studied in various aspects. Many scholars discussed the role of time in the forward sale and lending (Saadallah 1994) and *the value of time* (A. U. F. Ahmad and Hassan 2006; Batcha 2009; Siddique and Rahim 2015). The relations among the concepts of the *discount rate*, *interest rate*, *rate of return*, and *time preference rate* were also evaluated for various purposes (Zarqa 1983; Khan 1991; Siddiqui 2006).

Although there is a distinction between the concepts of the time value of money and time preference, they are considered highly relevant and usually evaluated together. It is the same in Islamic economics. The views of Islamic economists on the role of time preference in the existence of interest are closely associated with their interpretation of the time value of money.

7.1.1 Time Value of Money

It is possible to classify the Islamic economists into three groups according to their view on the concept of the time value of money. The deniers of the validity of the time value of money are the first group. The conditional acceptors and the full acceptors of the validity of time value are the other two groups.

7.1.1.1 The Rejecters

Some Islamic economists do not accept that the time has a value. M. Umer Chapra (2015), for example, explicitly notes that, according to Islam, the time passed in a loan transaction does not deserve any compensation by itself. According to Mohamed Fairooz Abdul Khir (2013), the primary reason for Islamic economists' not legitimizing the validity of the time value of money is about its role in the justification of interest in lending. Legitimizing it is considered a cause of legitimizing the validity of interest.

7.1.1.2 The Conditional Acceptors

Another group admits the existence and significance of the time value of money, but claim that it is only valid in commercial transactions (A. U. F. Ahmad and Hassan 2006; Ayub 2007; Batcha 2009; Askari et al. 2015;

Siddique and Rahim 2015). There are some other conditions asserted for the acceptance of the validity of the time value of money (Khan 1991; Kahf 1994).

Abu Umar F. Ahmad and M. Kabir Hassan (2006) accepted the existence of time value in pricing assets. According to them, the forward sale of a commodity at a price higher than its spot price is legitimate. Nevertheless, they claimed that a loan transaction could not include an increment in debt for time value.

According to Azah Atikah B. A. Batcha (2009), there is a general acceptance on the issue that the forward price of a commodity may be higher than its spot price, implying the validity of the time value of money. However, she also noted that since money is not a commodity but a medium of exchange, the interest received from lending is not possible to be considered as the difference between spot and forward prices of capital. Similarly, Muhammad Ayub (2007) wrote that the validity of time value is recognized in Islam but only in trade transactions, mentioning the difference between the spot and forward prices. According to him, it is not possible to value the time in loan transactions.

The assertion of Askari et al. (2015) was very similar to others that Islam accepts the concept of the time value of money with some restrictions. Although time value is legitimated in sales contracts, time does not deserve any compensation in loan transactions. Time alone does not produce anything but has a productive role in investment. Then, the capital used in economic activity receives some part of the income. They noted, on the other hand, that interest may inevitably be the result of the time value of money, but this does not mean it is fair.

Muhammad Abubakar Siddique and Memoona Rahim (2015) also considered time value to be valid in trade but refused its legitimacy in loan transactions. Differently, they introduced the concept of the *time value of commodity*, referring to the difference between the spot and forward prices. They stated that the time value of money is not valid while the *time value of commodity* is acceptable.

A different stipulation for the validity of time value was asserted by Fahim Khan (1991). He stated that Islam accepts the validity of the time value of money but constraints it to a case that the value is not defined in advance. Monzer Kahf (1994) did also support the thought of Islam's recognition of the validity of the time value of money. Still, differently, he raised the issue that the emergence of the licit value is revenue from investment, but it is not a reward of postponing the present consumption.

7.1.1.3 The Acceptors

The third group of Islamic economists legitimates the validity of the time value of money without the abovementioned stipulations. A quite distinct approach to the concept of the time value of money was showed by Rafic Yunus Al-Masri (2004). He pointed out that the difference between the spot and forward prices in a deferred sale is the time value of money, and it is allowed in Islamic economics. According to him, the origins of the time value of money and interest are the same, and they are both legitimate in Islamic law. Moreover, he highlighted a problem that emerged with the approach of Islamic economists. Although they are the same, the time value is called *profit* in deferred sales and *interest* in lending. In both Islamic and conventional economics, usually, profit is not intervened, but interest is controlled by the use of either administrative arrangements or financial instruments. Thus, neglecting the importance and usefulness of the time value and allowing it to be considered as the profit of deferred sale would cause very high, usurious interest rates.

An approach similar to Al-Masri (2004) was shown by Mahmoud A. El-Gamal (2006). He stated that although major jurisprudence schools accepted the validity of the time value of money, many Islamic economists did not admit it. Actually, according to him, the existence of legitimized instruments based on the difference between spot and forward prices validates the time value of money.

The approaches of the three groups of Islamic economists to the time value of money are presented in Table 7.1.

7.1.2 Time Preference in Islamic Economics

The views of the Islamic economists on the concept of time preference are highly diversified, and comprehensive analysis of the issue from an aspect of mainstream thought of Islamic economics is still missing. Since the significant distinction of Islamic economics from the conventional ones is being an interest-free system, the theories of interest, particularly the time preference theory as the most assertive one, would be expected to scrutinize. Various scholars dealt with the issue, and some of them worked on it in detail. However, the relevant works are not comprehensive enough to help in building an opinion on whether time preference can be the cause of interest or not.

Table 7.1 The approaches of Islamic economists to the time value of money

Group	*Basic approach*
Rejecters	Time has no value of money *e.g., M. Umer Chapra* (2015)
Conditional acceptors	Time has a value of money, but only in deferred sale transactions, not in lending *e.g., Ahmad and Hassan* (2006), *Ayub* (2007), *Siddique and Rahim* (2015)
	Time has a value of money, but only for the cases, which the value is not defined previously *e.g., Khan* (1991)
	Time has a value of money, but it is a return of investment; it does not arise from postponing the present consumption *e.g., Kahf* (1994)
Acceptors	Time has a value of money *e.g., Al-Masri* (2004), *El-Gamal* (2006)

It is remarkable and worthwhile to note that Böhm-Bawerk is not referred to or mentioned in many of the works dealing with time preference in the context of Islamic economics. Not being aware of Böhm-Bawerk's theory may imply that Islamic economists did not consider the inherent causes of time preference adequately.

Finally, there might be a misconception or undervaluing of the causes of time preference asserted by Böhm-Bawerk in the relevant literature. Some of the scholars who cited Böhm-Bawerk did partially refer to the claimed reasons for time preference.

Some scholars do not accept the generality of positive time preference. Another group refuses any cause-effect relation between positive time preference and a positive interest rate. On the other hand, some others consider positive time preference as a typical human attitude.

7.1.2.1 The Rejecters of the Generality of Positive Time Preference

Mahmud Ahmad and Iqbal Qureshi were two of the earliest Muslim scholars that commented on the theories of interest. In 1946, a relatively early time, Mahmud Ahmad (1975) reviewed existing theories of interest and attempted to refute them all. He specifically cited Böhm-Bawerk's assertion of people's attribution more value to present goods and claimed that Böhm-Bawerk's approach was an underestimation of universal reality. According to him, people's savings are made for rainy day needs without expecting any profit from them. On the contrary, anybody with income under the subsistence level is unable to save at any interest rate, any high interest rate cannot help to recover, and only in such a case, present goods may be preferred to future goods.

Concurrently with Mahmud Ahmad, Iqbal Qureshi (1946), another Islamic economist, stated that Böhm-Bawerk's significant contribution to the theory was the concept of the time-consuming characteristic of production and the role of capital in long processes. He introduced the time preference theory and admitted the technical superiority of present goods in production. However, he refused the validity of the psychological, subjective causes asserted by Böhm-Bawerk. Qureshi claimed that most people save as provision for future needs, which will be more vital than present ones due to their children's education and marriage, or requirements of old ages, etc.

Contrary to other Islamic economists, who mostly considered the consumption-relevant causes of time preference to be invalid, Muhammad Uzair (1976), interestingly, opposed Böhm-Bawerk's third cause, the technical superiority of present goods, and defined it to be a formidable assertion. He accused Böhm-Bawerk of his explanation of the capital formation and the roundaboutness of production. According to him, Böhm-Bawerk's assertion accounts for the accumulation of capital goods in primitive society but not provides any rationale for charging interest for the usage of the capital.

If it was not inattention, or he did not consciously ignore the first two causes, evaluating Böhm-Bawerk's assertion of the cause of time preference only by the use of the technical superiority of present goods is a misconception of Uzair. On the other hand, more importantly, aside from the accuracy of the evaluation on the role of roundaboutness that is confined to the accumulation of capital goods in a primitive society, it seems that Uzair overlooked the importance of the availability of capital goods in time-consuming production at present. The capital's role had never been crucial as it is at today due to ever-increasing large-scale production.

While reviewing the theories of interest from the aspect of factors of production in his work, Shamim Siddiqui (1996) stated that Böhm-Bawerk's theory was sophisticated, and the first two causes he asserted were subjective. In contrast, he defined the last cause of producing more in the future due to the roundabout process to be objective. However, he did not make any further comments about the validity of the causes.

After ten years, Siddiqui (2006), this time, reviewed the literature regarding the relation of time preference with interest rate. While summarizing Böhm-Bawerk's theory, he only considered the second cause of time preference that Böhm-Bawerk asserted. He stressed the underestimation of the future as the reason for time preference and kept the other two reasons apart. Siddiqui examined the claimed second cause in detail, presented scenarios, and stated that people's choice might change due to certainty, the security of savings, inflation, change in needs, expectation of future income, and investment opportunities. He concluded that positive time preference due to underestimation of the future is not a general human attitude. He refuted Böhm-Bawerk's assertion of people's lack of future imagination or weakness of will and claimed that people are generally rational in valuing their future. According to Siddiqui, the present income may be preferred compared to future income. However, it has not to be for a preference for current consumption, and this cannot be a justification for a reward of loan interest.

Tarek El Diwany (2011) objected to the concept of the underestimation of the future in Böhm-Bawerk's theory. He did not comment on the other two causes and stated that individuals prefer future pleasure to present pleasure in many cases. He asks why anybody should prefer to use the capital for consumption at present rather than the future unless she has a coercive reason to consume now.

7.1.2.2 The Deniers of the Relation of Positive Time Preference with Interest

Since the interest rate is used in discounting the future, zero interest rate policy creates a problem in such operations. While attempting to solve the problem, Anas Zarqa (1983) examined the nature of time preference in detail and asserted that the existence of a positive interest rate does not require a positive time preference. According to him, despite the lack of positive time preference, the productivity of capital would be enough to cause a positive interest rate. Besides, he claimed that the existence of time preference would not cause a positive interest rate unless it is legally permitted in the market. Zarqa objected to the assumption of the generality of positive time preference and attempted to show that non-positive time preference is also a rational human attitude by presenting examples of various cases. He concluded that as being not dominantly positive, time preference is not always the cause of discounting future benefits and losses.

A misconception on the concept of time preference may have caused Zarqa to consider the productivity of capital distinct from time preference. Essentially, the causes of time preference were defined to be relevant to the choice of either consuming more at present or employing the capital in production to consume more in the future (Böhm-Bawerk 1903). In other words, not only the preference of consuming more at present but also the productivity of capital is in the scope of time preference. On the other hand, when time preference technically tends to cause a positive interest rate, it would not be realistic to claim that the existence of interest can be entirely prevented in society by law or any other instrument.

Omar Zubair, one of the discussants of Zarqa's assertion, supported Zarqa's view and stated that there is no pure time preference in Islamic thought (Zarqa 1983). He stressed that approving the existence of time preference leads to validation of riba, and that time has a role only in the productivity of capital.

Monzer Kahf (1994) made a distinct assertion that time preference might be plausible for the saver whose capital is employed in production, and the return of the investment can only be determined at the end of the investment period.

The condition set by Kahf for the plausibility of time preference is hard to rationalize for two reasons. Firstly, such a distinction between savings used for investment and lending may be significant in legitimizing the income from the capital. Still, the dependence of the existence and plausibility of time preference on how the savings used is untenable. Secondly, although it is right that the income from an investment becomes evident when the outcome is acquired, it is not possible to decide whether to save or not in advance without a prediction of return rate.

7.1.2.3 The Acceptors of Positive Time Preference as a Common Attitude

Sultan Abu Ali, one of the discussants of Zarqa's (1983) assertion mentioned above, objected to Zarqa's approach to time preference (Zarqa 1983). He accused Zarqa of disregarding the existence of time preference and claimed that it was a reality, even in Muslim societies, and abolishing interest would not suppress its presence. Similarly, Ziauddin Ahmed (Zarqa 1983) stated that, since Islam is based on inherent attitudes, the human being could have a positive time preference, and believing in positive time preference is not wrong.

M. Fahim Khan (1991) stated the connection between the time value of money and the time preference and evaluated their relevance to the other two concepts: interest rate and rate of return. According to him, the assumption of a zero time preference was not justified in many works of Muslim scholars on the investment attitude of people, and the existence of positive time preference is plausible. Assuming the present consumption is always preferred to future consumption, future values are discounted by using interest rates as a proxy of the discount rate. Then, the interest rate may be a measure of time preference, which is determined in advance. Consumers use the interest rate in decision making for utility maximization by either consuming now or postponing the consumption for investment.

Khan pointed out that a problem would emerge in the absence of interest, and sought a solution for the case that neither an interest rate nor a predetermined time value of money is allowed to use as a time preference rate. A proposed measure to use as a proxy for the time value of money is capital's average rate of return that is not possible to determine precisely in advance due to uncertainty. The ex-post rate of return that is also including the time-relevant risk may be a measure for the time preference rate.

Regarding the validity of time preference, El-Gamal (2006) asserted that the findings in Loewenstein and Prelec's (1992) work about discounting the future benefits and losses were consistent with the human behavior described by many verses in the Quran. He underlined the observation within the abovementioned work that time preference is not only a determiner of choice between present and future time, but it also determines the choice between two distinct times that are both in the future.

Ayub (2007) asserted that there is not any justification for the generality of zero time preference. According to him, positive time preference is the universal human attitude.

Abdul Khir (2013) stated that the time value of money is relevant to the concept of time preference, and the positive time preference justifies the existence of a positive interest rate in conventional economics. He emphasized that Islam's prohibition of interest does not mean the presence of positive time preference is rejected.

The views of the three groups of Islamic economists on the concept of time preference are summarized in Table 7.2.

Table 7.2 The views of Islamic economists on the concept of time preference

Group	*Basic approach*
Rejecters of its generality	Positive time preference is not a common attitude *e.g., Qureshi* (1946), *Ahmad* (1975), *Siddiqui* (2006)
Rejecters of its relation with interest	The existence of a positive interest rate does not require a positive time preference *e.g., Zarqa* (1983)
Acceptors	Positive time preference is a typical attitude *e.g., Sultan Abu Ali, Ziauddin Ahmed* (Zarqa 1983), *Khan* (1991), *El-Gamal* (2006), *Abdul Khir* (2013)

7.1.3 Islamic Economists, Böhm-Bawerk's Theory, and the Time Value of Money

The most remarkable criticism against Böhm-Bawerk's theory is about the validity of the causes of time preference. Although there are objections to each of the three causes, more attempts have been made to refute the first two. The controversy is on the generality of the first two causes that refer to the preference of present goods to future ones for consumption. Specifically, the second cause, underestimation of the future, is mentioned. Scholars presented examples of cases causing negative or zero time preference.

It seems that there is a misconception about the first two causes of time preference. The theory did not claim that each individual always has a reason to value present goods higher than the future ones. There may be many cases in that present goods are saved without any expectation of increment in the value. Even in some cases, a payment may be made for postponement of current consumption to the future that refers to negative time preference. However, the existence of individuals with zero or negative time preference does not have any effect on the attitude of others with positive time preference. Each individual makes her own decision about consuming a good or saving it. For an individual with positive time preference, the necessary condition to postpone the consumption is a convincing increment in the savings depending on the time passed. The increment may be either a profit or an interest.

On the other hand, in a case that the amount of the savings of individuals with zero or negative time preference increases much, and such savings are put on the loan market, the price of capital may dramatically decrease. Consequently, individuals with positive time preference would give up saving due to the reduced return on capital. However, this does not imply any change in their choice of present goods. Above all, the domination of zero or negative time preference that is causing a non-positive interest rate is an exceptional case, which is observed during recessions.

Lastly, it is noticed that the legitimacy of Böhm-Bawerk's third cause of time preference, namely the technical superiority of present goods, is more widely accepted among Islamic economists compared to other reasons. Although the third cause does not refer to the productivity theory of interest, considering it as such may be the reason for the broader acceptance of the validity of this cause. Since the favorable role of an earlier possessed capital in production is widely approved, it is easier to justify the preference of present goods for production than explaining the other two causes. Moreover, in Islamic economics, there is a valid, plausible, and even encouraged instrument used in capital utilization: partnership based on profit-loss sharing legitimizes the expectation of a reward from the employment of capital.

Concerning the concept of the time value of money, most of the Islamic Economists' evaluations about the validity of the time value do not appear as the outcomes of methodological analyses. They seem to be guided by their belief in the evilness of interest. It is concerned that the unconditional acceptance of the validity of the time value of money would inevitably legitimize interest. Therefore, time is defined to have value only in credit sale transactions, referring to the difference between spot and future prices. Consequently, various instruments were developed by grounding on the legitimacy of the mentioned difference, and they were mostly used as substitutes for the prohibited interest-based transactions.

However, unfortunately, it has to be stated that the difference between the spot and future prices of an item is regarded as interest in conventional economics, and most of the instruments based on forward sale have the same consequences as interest-based transactions have. Besides, the forward sale based interest-free instruments are more costly than conventional borrowing.

7.2 Consideration of Interest Rate Control in Islamic Economics Literature

The response of Islamic economists to the assertive time preference theory, which implies the inevitableness of interest, is not satisfactory enough. Unfortunately, the issue of the consequences of interest rate control has received far less attention compared to the concept of time preference among Islamic economists.

Price control as an economic conception has been worked on to an extent in Islamic economics both by the old jurists and the contemporary Islamic economists (Kamali 1994; Bashar 1997; Ghazanfar and Islahi 2003). From the beginning, the intervention of authorities in price formation in the market has been discussed in many aspects. Not only its legitimacy and the conditions that it becomes useful or necessary, but the results of price control were also studied.

The unfairness of fixing or limiting price for the seller unless there is a plausible reason was one of the first raised issues. It was presented that the shortage, a result of price control, distorts the market and guides people to black-market; the sellers are discouraged from staying in the market, and the number of exchanges decreases (Bashar 1997). The decision-makers were warned about the undermining effect of excessive controls on people's profit motive (Ghazanfar and Islahi 2003).

However, the scope of the works on price control has not been extended enough, covering the controls on the price of capital, namely interest rate control. Many Islamic economists studied and wrote on the implications of abolishing interest, but almost all of them mentioned only the feasibility and positive effects of abolition.

Among a few Muslim scholars dealt with adverse effects of interest rate control on the market, Fazlur Rahman's evaluation was the most extensive one. Although he did not scrutinize the issue in all aspects, Rahman (1964) touched on many market distortive effects of abolishing interest by referring to the approach of conventional economics. He pointed out that since the interest rate is a price, it operates according to the same mechanisms that price has. Rahman described the emergence of shortage due to zero interest rate, limited supply of, and infinite demand for capital. He stressed the problem of rationing the available capital to be loaned in a society with nepotism and corruption. Rahman asserted that, with interest at market rates, namely, when capital is neither too cheap nor too expensive, the loan would be received by appropriate borrowers. He disagreed with the economists claiming the possibility of equating interest rate to zero by administrative regulation. He pleaded that the interest rate would decrease near to zero itself in an economy only if wealth and capital increase enough to an extent where the supply of and demand for the loan are almost equalized.

Anas Zarqa (1982) cited Samuelson's assertion of the conditions for zero interest rate. In the case of perfect certainty, the zero interest rate is possible only if capital is saturated. In a real situation of uncertainty, the interest rate may decrease to zero due to recession. However, Zarqa claimed that when an authority establishes a zero interest rate ceiling, the interest-based loan market would be eliminated, but an active equity market might be an alternative. Zarqa mentioned nothing about any adverse consequences of the prohibition of interest. Still, he asserted that the rate of return within the equity market as a price signal might be used in the allocation of capital. There is no need to concern about growth and the efficiency of the market for the absence of interest. Because, as he claimed, interest-free allocation improves efficiency, and not using interest has no adverse effect on savings, investment, and innovation, so on growth.

Then, Zarqa (1983) evaluated the role of discounting in economics and the relation of interest with discount rate. He stated that discounting is needed for efficient investment, and the discount rate is considered dependent on the interest rate in conventional economics. He stressed the problem of defining the discount rate in the absence of interest and proposed to use the rate of return on equity as a discount rate.

A few more scholars, although not profoundly analyzed the consequences of the prohibition of interest, focused on the required conditions for successfully abolishing it. Syed Nawab Haider Naqvi and Asghar Qadir (1986) discussed the implications of abolition, and they stated that if the capital is not saturated, it is not possible to abolish interest by regulations unless alternative instruments that would take over the role of interest are established. They showed that in such a case, the capital would depreciate due to its expending.

The findings of Naqvi and Qadir were presented again by Naqvi (2013) but this time more extensively. He stated that according to Islamic ethical principles, any regulation made in the economic system has to consider efficiency and equality. Therefore, arrangements such as the abolition of interest should not adversely affect the total wealth and not make the income distribution worse. Besides, any instrument established as an alternative to interest-based ones should not remove the small investors from the market. In this frame, he claimed that abolishing interest at once without building a replacement would not be an appropriate solution because the capital with a zero price, namely the capital in a market with zero interest rate, would be consumed. It is so because the marginal utility of consumption exponentially increases in such a case implying that the marginal utility of saving decreases to a minimum.

References

Abdul Khir, Mohamed Fairooz. 2013. "The Concept of the Time Value of Money: A Shari'ah Viewpoint." *International Journal of Excellence in Islamic Banking and Finance* 3 (2): 1–15.

Ahmad, Mahmud. 1975. *İslam Iktisadı: Mukayeseli Bir Tedkik* [Economics of Islam: A Comparative Study]. İstanbul: Cağaloğlu Yayınevi.

Ahmad, Abu Umar Faruq, and M. Kabir Hassan. 2006. "The Time Value of Money Concept in Islamic Finance." *American Journal of Islamic Social Sciences* 23 (1): 66.

Al-Masri, Rafic Yunus. 2004. "Are All Forms of Interest Prohibited?" *Journal of King Abdulaziz University: Islamic Economics* 17 (1): 37–41.

Askari, Hossein, Zamir Iqbal, and Abbas Mirakhor. 2015. *Introduction to Islamic Economics: Theory and Application*. Singapore: Wiley.

Ayub, Muhammad. 2007. *Understanding Islamic Finance*. Wiley Finance Series. Hoboken, NJ: Wiley.

Bashar, Muhammad Lawal Ahmad. 1997. "Price Control in an Islamic Economy." *Journal of King Abdulaziz University: Islamic Economics* 9: 29–52.

Batcha, Azah Atikah Binti Anwar. 2009. *Time Value of Money and Riba: Islamic Perspective*. Kuala Lumpur: INCEIF.

Böhm-Bawerk, Eugen. 1903. *Recent Literature on Interest (1884–1899): A Supplement to "Capital and Interest."* New York: Macmillan.

Chapra, Muhammad Umer. 2015. *Prohibition of Interest: Does It Make Sense*. Durban: Islamic Dawah Movement.

El Diwany, Tarek. 2011. *Faiz Sorunu* [The Problem with Interest]. İstanbul: İz Yayıncılık.

El-Gamal, Mahmoud A. 2006. "An Attempt to Understand the Economic Wisdom (Hikma) in the Prohibition of Riba." In *Interest in Islamic Economics Understanding Riba*, edited by Abdulkadir Thomas, 111–23. New York: Routledge.

Ghazanfar, Shaikh M., and Abdul Azim Islahi. 2003. "Explorations in Medieval Arab-Islamic Economic Thought—Some Aspects of Ibn Taimiyah's Economics." In *Medieval Islamic Economic Thought—Filling the Great Gap in European Economics*, edited by Shaikh M. Ghazanfar, 53–71. Rouledge-Curzon.

Kahf, Monzer. 1994. "Time Value of Money and Discounting in Islamic Perspective: Re-Visited." *Review of Islamic Economics* 3 (2): 31–38.

Kamali, Mohamad Hashim. 1994. "'Tas'ir' (Price Control) in Islamic Law." *American Journal of Islamic Social Sciences* 11 (1): 25–37.

Khan, M. Fahim. 1991. "Time Value of Money and Discounting in Islamic Perspective." *Review of Islamic Economics* 1 (2): 35–45.

Loewenstein, George, and Drazen Prelec. 1992. "Anomalies in Intertemporal Choice: Evidence and an Interpretation." *The Quarterly Journal of Economics* 107 (2): 573–97.

Naqvi, Syed Nawab Haider. 2013. *Islam, Economics, and Society*. New York: Routledge.

Naqvi, Syed Nawab Haider, and Asghar Qadir. 1986. *A Model of a Dynamic Islamic Economy and the Institution of Interest*. Essays in Islamic Economic Philosophy 4. Islamabad: Pakistan Institute of Development Economics.

Qureshi, Iqbal. 1946. *Islam and the Theory of Interest*. Lahore: Sh. M. Ashraf.

Rahman, Fazlur. 1964. "Riba and Interest." *Islamic Studies* 3 (1): 1–43.

Saadallah, Ridha. 1994. "Concept of Time in Islamic Economics." *Islamic Economic Studies* 2 (1): 81–102.

Siddique, Muhammad Abubakar, and Memoona Rahim. 2015. "The Concepts of Discounting and Time Value of Money in Islamic Capital Budgeting Framework: A Theoretical Study." *Journal of Islamic Banking and Finance* 32 (1): 23–29.

Siddiqui, Shamim Ahmad. 1996. "Factors of Production and Factor Returns under Political Economy of Islam." *Journal of King AbdulAziz University: Islamic Economics* 8 (1): 3–28.

———. 2006. "The Controversy over Time Value of Money among Contemporary Muslim Economists." *Journal of Management and Social Sciences* 2 (2): 144–53.

Uzair, Muḥammad. 1976. "Some Conceptual and Practical Aspects of Interest-Free Banking." *Islamic Studies* 15 (4): 247–69.

Zarqa, Muhammad Anas. 1982. "Capital Allocation, Efficiency and Growth in an Interest-Free Islamic Economy." *Journal of Economics and Administration, King Abdulaziz University* 16: 43–55.

———. 1983. "An Islamic Perspective on the Economics of Discounting in Project Evaluation." In *Fiscal Policy and Resource Allocation in Islam*, edited by Ziauddin Ahmed, Munawar Iqbal, and M. Fahim Khan, 179–223. Jeddah: International Centre for Research in Islamic Economics, King Abdulaziz University.

CHAPTER 8

Conclusion

The *interest*, with different definitions and dimensions, has been a reality of human life throughout almost all known history. In the beginning, presumably, at the time of the first farmers, it was an issue of the people that needed seed at sowing time but could not borrow from a relative or a friend on a charity or cooperation basis. The alternative was borrowing from someone else and paying back more at harvest time. Afterward, the scope of lending was widened, and some other goods, the commodities that were used as money, and finally, the money itself began to be lent.

The word *interest* was used literally in various meanings previously in Europe, but it refers to almost the same thing in English since the sixteenth century ("Interest in Online Etymology Dictionary" 2019): *payment for the use of borrowed money*. At times that interest was not allowed to practice; all interest-bearing loans were defined to be usurious. The distinction between the meanings of usury and interest-bearing lending was made after the removal of the prohibition of interest at rates not exceeding a defined limit in Europe.

On the other hand, regarding its term meaning in economics, although interest is defined as an income received from capital as a factor of production, some scholars preferred to differentiate its coverage. According to Fisher (1930), all types of income are interest, and Schumpeter (1934) defined it as the name of all returns except wages. Of course, regardless of how it is described, interest always exists with capital. Therefore,

C. Eyerci, *The Causes and Consequences of Interest Theory*, https://doi.org/10.1007/978-3-030-78702-8_8

Böhm-Bawerk (1890) preferred the definition as *the income that flows from capital is interest.*

It would not be wrong to state that the role of interest in the economy has never been as extensive as its role during the last century, specifically the last few decades. Evolved economic life due to the new characteristics of all relevant fields on both production and consumption sides of the economy and the financialization of the societies made the concept of interest one of the focused issues of daily life. Today, interest is not only a simple phenomenon of ordinary loan transactions. Besides the numerous types of sophisticated and exhaustive loan transactions, it is utilized in many other fields such as commercial transactions, planning activities, discounting in budgeting, and project evaluation.

However, it must also be admitted that interest has attracted intense attention, which it exceedingly deserved. Although not achieved consensus on many relevant issues, the concept of interest has been thought, studied, and discussed by philosophers, religious scholars, lawmakers, administrators, and economists, of course, regarding almost all economic, social, moral, and religious aspects. The goodness, beneficialness, necessity, legitimacy, licitness, honorableness, respectability, charitableness of interest have always been disputed. There has been much debate about whether it should be lawful or illegal, or should be freed, limited, or prohibited. Each scholar attempted to justify her assertion within the scope of her profession. Any declaration on interest was originated from religious beliefs, ethical principles, social needs, or economic considerations, or a combination of these.

The legitimacy of interest-based lending was one of the points that debate concentrated. Interest was considered a sin (Visser and McIntosh 1998), and condemned for being dishonorable, disrespectable, uncharitable, and unjust (Homer 1963; Olechnowicz 2011; Graeber 2011). It was thought that interest is the source of many evils such as earning without working, exploiting the needy, causing economic instability, guiding people to materialism, decreasing the tendency to entrepreneurship (Durkin 1993; Rougeau 1996; Visser and McIntosh 1998; Sharawy 2000; DeLorenzo 2006; Muhammad Farooq 2012; Erdem 2018). Almost all the claimed negativities of interest are concerns of more than one source of motivation. Exploiting the needy is a religious, ethical, social, and economic problem, for example. Earning without working is a sin and not moral. Similarly, inequality in wealth distribution is not desired in both religions and economics.

Therefore, interest-based lending has always been regulated by the authorities. Many laws and administrative arrangements were used in regulations since the ancient times such as the Sumerian legal code (Vincent 2014), Code of Hammurabi in Babylonia (Homer 1963), Laws of Manu in ancient India (Visser and McIntosh 1998), Solon's Laws of ancient Greece, Twelve Tables of ancient Rome, and Justinian's Code of Byzantium (Homer 1963).

In various societies, lending at interest was entirely prohibited in some periods. However, the more prevalent arrangement was allowing interest with limited rates. The permitted interest rates were highly diversified due to various factors that are still the determiners of the interest rates in modern times, such as the time, place, maturity, size, the legality of the loan; the reliability and the neediness of the borrower; the identity of the lender; and the existence of indemnity for the loan. The interest limits for standard loans were in a range of 20–33½% per annum in ancient Mesopotamia (Homer 1963); 15–60% in ancient India (Graeber 2011); 4⅙–48% in ancient Greece; 4–12% in ancient Rome (Homer 1963). There were loans made at an interest rate well below the declared limits in all societies. Still, some examples were exceeding the legal limits up to usurious levels, 9000% in ancient Greece, for instance (Homer 1963).

It is interesting to observe that there could be a distinction among the interest rates in lending of different goods. In ancient Mesopotamia, for example, barley was lending at an interest rate of 33½% per annum, but the interest rate for a loan of silver was 20% (Homer 1963). Presumably, the reason for the distinction was the expectation of a natural decrease in the price of barley at the harvest time.

The legal arrangements did not only control the interest rates by defining limits. Many established rules determined the ways of the registration of loans, the consequences of not obeying the relevant regulations, the assets to be used for indemnity, the enforcement methods in the execution of loan contracts, and the sanctions in case of default.

Along with the regulations valid for long terms, in extraordinary cases, the authorities made ad-hoc interventions to the interest-based lending transactions. For various social reasons such as providing justice and equity and protecting the widows and orphans, the imprisoned or slaved people for not paid debt were freed, and the debts were canceled or reduced several times in various societies (Homer 1963; Graeber 2011; Vincent 2014).

The regulations of interest have been survived until the modern days. Even today, lending at interest is entirely prohibited by law in some countries. In some others, there are interest rate ceilings (Glaeser and Scheinkman 1994; Reifner et al. 2010) aiming to prevent usurious transactions.

In the regulation of the practice of interest, the used instruments were not only the laws and administrative decisions. The financial arrangements have also been useful in the control of interest. The authorities themselves or other institutions such as temples lent to needy people at lower than market rates, even free of interest (Homer 1963). The interventions of the central banks through the reserve requirement ratios are a contemporary example (Reifner et al. 2010) for financial instruments.

On the other hand, religion and morality were not only the origin of the thoughts on interest but also providing some instruments used in the enforcement of the relevant regulations. The religions' consideration of interest as a sin and the societies' view of the ethical inconvenience of interest helped to enforce the rules, to an extent. Christianity, Islam, and, with some exceptions, Judaism prohibited lending at interest at the beginning (Visser and McIntosh 1998; Küçükkalay 2018).

However, the most observed change in the view of authorities on the legitimacy of interest was in Christian Europe. After surviving for centuries with minor changes in its scope, and enforcement and sanctioning ways (Homer 1963), in the sixteenth century, the prohibition of interest was relaxed gradually by the emergence of Protestantism. A century later, the increased need for finance due to the development of trade made the role of interest in the economy more significant. Finally, usury was redefined in the non-Catholic regions as lending at interest higher than the acceptable rate (Visser and McIntosh 1998). The Catholic Church's adoption of the new approach came in the nineteenth century. As it is still the Church's view (Visser and McIntosh 1998), taking an interest not more than the defined limit was allowed for everybody (Homer 1963). However, it must be noted that the concept of *an acceptable interest rate* is a much-debated issue, it is not clear, and there is not a consensus on it.

Another controversial field within the debate of the legitimacy of interest was about its nature. Although it was not a new issue, this time by the eighteenth century, the debaters were mostly economists, and they dealt specifically with the economic aspects of interest in a more scientific way. The scholars tried to understand the nature of interest, namely the reason for its existence, first; then, its effect, necessity, fairness, usefulness, and goodness (Böhm-Bawerk 1890). Many economists developed either monetary or nonmonetary theories of interest that had similarities and discrepancies, focused on various aspects of the issue, and mainly tried to present the cause of the existence of interest.

Among all other scholars, Eugen von Böhm-Bawerk, who was introduced as the founder of the modern theory of interest (Conard 1959; Potuzak 2016), had an unusual approach for several reasons. The striking assertion he made was the distinction between the positive and normative aspects of the concept of interest. He did not use the words *positive* and *normative*. Still, he claimed that the cause of the existence of interest, which is an issue of the positive domain, should be worked apart from all other normative aspects of the social and political fields. He explicitly criticized the theories up to him (Böhm-Bawerk 1890, 1903) and claimed that the main reason for the fallacies in those works was not making the abovementioned distinction (Böhm-Bawerk 1890).

Then, Böhm-Bawerk presented his comprehensive theory of interest (Böhm-Bawerk 1930) that was integrated with a theory of capital. The emphasis he made on the vital role of capital in time-consuming production processes is another crucial contribution he made to the literature (Qureshi 1946). The abovementioned role of capital is not only considered in the evaluation of the cause of interest. It is also discussed in the interpretation of profit (Böhm-Bawerk 1890) and the valuation of the product of labor (Böhm-Bawerk 1930).

There have always been concerns about the harmfulness of interest. Many legislative and administrative regulations prohibiting interest or limiting its rate have been in effect, almost all over the world historically. However, whether it was allowed or not, interest-based transactions were, more or less, always existed (Kuran 1995). The existence of interest-bearing lending, despite its prohibition in Europe and the Muslim world, was either through loopholes in the law or illegal ways (Visser and McIntosh 1998).

Following the controversies on the issues of the legitimacy of the existence of interest and the cause of interest, a further disagreement is about whether interest rate control, namely prohibiting interest or limiting its rate, is serving the purpose or not. Although the regulations of interest are highly prevalent and many scholars are supporting the necessity and usefulness of interest rate control; in theory, most of the economists are opposed to any prohibition or limitation of interest (Durkin 1993) considering its distortive effects on the market.

As being a form of price control, interest rate control may have similar undesired consequences, as price control has in general. Shortages or excess supply, queues, bribing, black-markets, reduction in economic activity and total welfare, reduction in the incentive to invest and to improve the quality of products are universal implications of controls that may be observed.

Moreover, the probable adverse results of the controls opposite to the intention should be evaluated well. Inflationary effects may be faced due to price control that is established to tackle inflation (Schuettinger and Butler 1979; Miller 2015). Wage floors, on the other hand, may make to find jobs impossible for the less qualified workers, contrary to its purpose of preventing workers, specifically the less qualified ones, from the exploitation of the employers. Similarly, although the wage floor aims equity in the workplace, it causes to pay the same wage to variously qualified workers (Siebert 2015).

The adverse effects in the loan market due to interest rate control may be more disturbing compared to the ones in other price controls. In case of a loan shortage, the lenders discriminate the risky borrowers from others, and the needier ones, who are also risky, cannot borrow. Although interest rate control is established to protect low-income consumers and weak businesses by aiming justice, the control policy may be a source of unfairness (Schmidtz 2016).

Coming back to the issue of the legitimacy of interest-based lending, evaluating the response of the opponents of interest to the assertions on the cause of interest and consequences of controlling may be purposeful. It is evident that there are many reasons claimed for the harmfulness of interest, and there is a demand to control it by prohibiting it or limiting its rate. On the other hand, others consider interest to be beneficial for the economy, present the cause of its existence as an inevitable and inherent human attitude and warn about the distortive consequences of controlling interest in the market.

Although some of the reasons for objecting to interest are originating from normative approaches, the relevant economists are increasingly attempting to justify their assertions in the positive domain. Therefore, interest opposing economists' approaches to the abovementioned two ambiguous issues would help in clarification. Since it is assertive and comprehensive, the implications of Böhm-Bawerk's time preference theory of interest on the economists are an appropriate indicator in evaluating their stance about the claimed cause of interest. The interpretation of the consequences of interest rate control by the interest-opponent economists is also essential. Refuting the claimed distortive effects of controls or accepting their validity has different implications on the thought of economics.

Among many others supporting interest rate controls, the economists demanding an interest-free economic system exhibit the most explicit attitude against interest. There is no doubt that the success of the proposed interest-free system and instruments developed within this system as well depends on the persuasiveness of their interpretations of these two issues to some extent.

It is focused on the approach of Islamic economics to scrutinize the abovementioned interpretations, rather than assessing the assertions of scholars from all interest-free economic systems. Studying Islamic economics as a representative of interest-free systems might not be wrong because the significant distinction of Islamic economics from the conventional ones is the prohibition of interest. Moreover, Islamic economics has active supporters among administrators, scholars, financial service providers; ever-increasing literature; a growing market; and actively operating interest-free instruments.

The society in which Islam emerged had a well-organized trade system operating on vast geography from Europe to Korea (Hamidullah 1980; Koehler 2014). The economic system based on trade had been active also after the emergence of Islamic belief with some modifications made according to Islamic principles. Along with economic life, many Muslim scholars of various disciplines continued working on economic thought until the fifteenth century. Then, thought disappeared almost in all fields, including economics, in the Muslim world for centuries (Chapra 2000).

An Islamic approach of economics reappeared by the independence of new Muslim countries after the Second World War (Chapra 2000), and particularly in the last few decades, applications of Islamic economics began to take place in the market. Although the share of Islamic finance assets in total world financial assets is only about 1% (Cohen 2017), its annual growth is 15% on average (Thomson Reuters 2018).

Islamic economic system is considered distinct from other systems (M. A. Khan 2013). Among some differences that mainly ground on Quran and Sunnah, the prohibition of interest is, presumably, the most significant one. There is no doubt that riba is explicitly prohibited (M. A. Khan

2013) both in Quran and in Sunnah. However, there has been a controversy on the meaning and nature of riba (Z. Ahmad 1978; Mohammad Farooq 2007) and its equivalence to interest.

Riba was a pre-Islamic practice and defined as the excessive increment in the debt, doubling or tripling, for example, when it was not paid on the date of maturity (Uludağ 1988), similar to today's penalty for delay or interest of default. There were not any rules or limitations for the rate of the increment, and the arbitrarily defined rate by the lender (Erdem 2018) frequently put the needy borrowers in misery.

Although not defined, the Quran explicitly prohibited riba, referring to its folded characteristic. The case in Sunnah is the same for the prohibition of riba, but the scope of riba in Sunnah is highly controversial. Some hadiths seem contradictory, which may be due to the lack of information about their contexts. On the other hand, some of the reported hadiths, including weak and even fabricated ones, were not reliable enough (Uludağ 1988).

The issue becomes more complicated in fiqh due to diversified thoughts of jurists about the interpretation and the scope of riba. There are differences in the conception of the hadiths and in methodologies of the jurists in making analogies. Above all, the lack of a uniformly accepted cause for the prohibition of riba (Deniz 2006) gives rise to further diversifications in analogies made.

After all, the most common interpretation of the evidence in the Quran and Sunnah dominated other different approaches, and the mainstream thought emerged: *Riba* was defined as *the addition to the principal lent and paid by the borrower to the lender for either the loan or an extension in the loan's maturity* (Chapra 2006). Accordingly, interest is considered as riba, and disregarding its type, purpose, size, and identity of the parties; it is prohibited.

Although the mainstream approach to riba has been the primary regulator of economic life, there have also been contrarians of the traditional view. Just from the beginning, some of the jurists, economists, and others approached the issue differently. They made various definitions for riba that mostly excluding some of the interest-based transactions from its scope.

Since the interest-based transactions were prohibited in Muslim societies, alternative instruments for capital utilization in investment were advanced. The most mentioned alternatives were based on the principle of profit-loss sharing and renting. On the other hand, to evade the prohibition of interest, although not legitimized by all jurists, some devious instruments were frequently used. Remarkably, most of these devious instruments were also used in Christian and Jew societies when interest was prohibited.

The approach of Islamic economists to the concept of time preference is scrutinized. It was observed that, besides evaluation of time preference, the Islamic economists worked on the role of time (Saadallah 1994) in economic life and on the concept of the time value of money (A. U. F. Ahmad and Hassan 2006; Batcha 2009; Siddique and Rahim 2015). The interrelations among the concepts of the discount rate, interest rate, rate of return, and time preference rate were also evaluated (Zarqa 1983; M. F. Khan 1991; Siddiqui 2006).

Although some scholars are refusing the time value of money, some others regard it to be valid, but usually, confine its validity only to sale transactions. According to them, time has no value in lending.

There are also some scholars legitimatizing the time value of money without any stipulations. Al-Masri (2004), one of these scholars raised an interesting issue that the profit in the deferred sale is not intervened while interest in lending is controlled in general. Therefore, although it is the same as interest, considering the time value of money as the profit of deferred sale would cause very high usurious interest rates.

The approaches of Islamic economists to the concept of time preference are highly diversified. However, although many scholars of Islamic economics studied on time preference or relevant issues, the need for a comprehensive scrutinizing of the concept of time preference from an aspect of traditional Islamic economics is not met.

Another noticeable issue within the works of Islamic economists is that there may be a misconception or undervaluing of the causes asserted by Böhm-Bawerk for time preference. Many of the works of Islamic economists on time preference do not refer to Böhm-Bawerk or mention him.

Many scholars accept the validity of time preference, but most of them refuse its generality of being positive. On the other hand, some others consider positive time preference as a typical human attitude.

Böhm-Bawerk's theory is mostly criticized for the validity of the first two causes, he asserted. Specifically, the second cause, underestimation of the future, is attempted to refute. The main objection is to the generality of the two causes that refer to the preference of present goods to future goods.

The theory does not state that each individual always has a reason to prefer present goods. There may be cases for any individual in which future goods are preferred or valued equal to present goods. However, the existence of individuals with zero or negative time preference does not make any change in the attitude of individuals with positive time preference. Each individual makes her own decision whether to consume now or to save for an increment.

The legitimacy of Böhm-Bawerk's third cause of time preference, the technical superiority of present goods, is accepted more compared to other causes. Although it is not, being considered as a form of productivity theory of interest might be a reason for the acceptance of the third cause. Since the positive role of an earlier possessed capital in production is widely accepted, it is easier to justify the preference of present goods for production compared to the other two reasons. Moreover, as a valid, plausible, and encouraged instrument in Islamic economics, profit-loss sharing is an appropriate way of capital utilization that legitimizes saving with an expectation of a reward from the employment of capital.

Although not satisfactory enough, the Islamic economists responded to the asserted causes of time preference theory. However, unfortunately, the issue of the consequences of interest rate control has received far less attention.

The concept of price control has been worked on to an extent, both by the old jurists and the contemporary Islamic economists (Kamali 1994; Bashar 1997; Ghazanfar and Islahi 2003). Not only its legitimacy and the conditions in that it becomes useful or necessary, but also the results of price control were also studied. However, the works on price control in Islamic economics have not been extended enough, covering the implications of interest rate control.

Many Islamic economists studied the consequences of abolishing interest, but almost all the work done was about the feasibility and beneficial effects of abolition. A few Muslim scholars dealt with the adverse effects of interest rate control on the market. They mostly attempted to define the required conditions that would prevent the emergence of adverse effects of abolishing interest, such as the depreciation of capital (Naqvi and Qadir 1986), decrease in total wealth, worsening in income distribution, and exclusion of small investors from the market (Naqvi

2013). Only Rahman (1964) presented many undesired distortive impacts of restrictions.

Zarqa presented the problems of difficulties in capital allocation (Zarqa 1982) and discounting (Zarqa 1983) in case of removing interest, and proposed to use the rate of return on equity instead of interest both in the allocation of capital and discounting.

The Islamic economic system is developed in line with the basic principles defined by the Quran, Sunnah, and decrees of Muslim jurists. Hence, the considerable part of the content of Islamic economics is normative, and the assertions of Islamic economists are mostly about desirable ideals. However, although it is hard to talk about a positive approach within the Islamic economic system today, it is possible to realize it by the use of convincing methodologies in testing its distinctive assertions. Reversely, the lack of successful implementations that are commonly held may be the reason for the normative aspects, which focus on the basic principles and ideals, coming into prominence more.

It has to be stated that the eternal problem of interest is still not resolved by the consensus of Muslim scholars. The Islamic economists did not respond adequately to the assertions regarding the causes, particularly time preference, that legitimate the existence of interest by claiming to ground on human nature.

On the other hand, any instrument that fully substitutes the function of interest without causing the claimed undesired or adverse consequences of its practice, and its control as well, could not be developed. Although it is considered otherwise in traditional Islamic economics, the difference between the spot and future prices of an item is regarded as interest in conventional economics, and the widely used instruments that are based on forward sale yield the same consequences as interest does. Moreover, most of these so-called interest-free instruments are more costly to the borrower than using interest.

Responding to the abovementioned challenge and searching for adequate alternative instruments requires a new approach to the issue that is mostly developed in the positive domain and supported by conceptual analysis and empirical studies. It is so because although the ideal models are useful in guiding human behavior, the communities pursue the factually working and operational prescriptions.

References

Ahmad, Ziauddin. 1978. "The Theory of Ribā." *Islamic Studies* 17 (4): 171–85.

Ahmad, Abu Umar Faruq, and M. Kabir Hassan. 2006. "The Time Value of Money Concept in Islamic Finance." *American Journal of Islamic Social Sciences* 23 (1): 66.

Al-Masri, Rafic Yunus. 2004. "Are All Forms of Interest Prohibited?" *Journal of King Abdulaziz University: Islamic Economics* 17 (1): 37–41.

Bashar, Muhammad Lawal Ahmad. 1997. "Price Control in an Islamic Economy." *Journal of King Abdulaziz University: Islamic Economics* 9: 29–52.

Batcha, Azah Atikah Binti Anwar. 2009. *Time Value of Money and Riba: Islamic Perspective*. Kuala Lumpur: INCEIF.

Böhm-Bawerk, Eugen. 1890. *Capital and Interest: A Critical History of Economical Theory*. London: The Macmillan Company.

———. 1903. *Recent Literature on Interest (1884–1899): A Supplement to "Capital and Interest."* New York: Macmillan.

———. 1930. *The Positive Theory of Capital*. New York: G.E.Stechert.

Chapra, Muhammad Umer. 2000. "Is It Necessary to Have Islamic Economics?" *The Journal of Socio-Economics* 29 (1): 21–37.

———. 2006. "The Nature of Riba in Islam." *Journal of Islamic Economics, Banking and Finance* 2 (1): 7–25.

Cohen, Suleiman Ibrahim. 2017. "Islamic Economics and Modern Economies: Resetting the Research Agenda." *Journal of Global Economics* 5 (2).

Conard, Joseph W. 1959. *An Introduction to the Theory of Interest*. Berkeley: University of California Press.

DeLorenzo, Yusuf Talal. 2006. "Introduction to Understanding Riba." In *Interest in Islamic Economics: Understanding Riba*, edited by Abdulkadir Thomas, 1–9. New York: Routledge.

Deniz, Abdülbaki. 2006. "İslam Hukukunda Illet Kavramı ve Faizin Illeti [Cause in Islamic Law and Cause of Interest]." Master Thesis, İstanbul: Uludağ University.

Durkin, Thomas A. 1993. "An Economic Perspective on Interest Rate Limitations." *Georgia State University Law Review* 9 (4).

Erdem, Ekrem. 2018. "Kur'an'da Riba (Faiz) Ayetlerinin Kademeli Nüzulü ve Üslubu: İslam'ın Ticaret, Infak ve Finans Sistemi Üzerinden Bir Inceleme [The Gradual Revelation and Style of the Riba (Interest) Verses in Quran: An Enquiry Regarding the Trade, Aid and Finance System of Islam]." In *İslam Iktisadı Perspektifinden Faiz* [Interest from the Perspective of Islamic Economics], edited by Taha Eğri and Zeynep Hafsa Orhan, 1–51. İstanbul: İktisat Yayınları.

Farooq, Mohammad. 2007. "The Riba-Interest Equivalence: Is There an Ijma (Consensus)?" *Transnational Dispute Management* 4 (5).

———. 2012. "Interest, Usury and Its Impact on the Economy." *Dialogue* 7 (3): 265–76.

Fisher, Irving. 1930. *The Theory of Interest*. New York: The Macmillan Company.

Ghazanfar, Shaikh M., and Abdul Azim Islahi. 2003. "Explorations in Medieval Arab-Islamic Economic Thought—Some Aspects of Ibn Taimiyah's Economics." In *Medieval Islamic Economic Thought—Filling the Great Gap in European Economics*, edited by Shaikh M. Ghazanfar, 53–71. Rouledge-Curzon.

Glaeser, Edward L., and Jose A. Scheinkman. 1994. "Neither a Borrower nor a Lender Be: An Economic Analysis of Interest Restrictions and Usury Laws." 4954. National Bureau of Economic Research.

Graeber, David. 2011. *Debt: The First 5000 Years*. New York: Melville House Publishing.

Hamidullah, Muhammed. 1980. *İslam Peygamberi* [The Prophet of Islam]. İstanbul: İrfan Yayınevi.

Homer, Sidney. 1963. *A History of Interest Rates*. New Brunswick, NJ: Rutgers University Press.

"Interest in Online Etymology Dictionary." 2019. https://www.etymonline.com/word/interest. Accessed on February 17, 2019.

Kamali, Mohamad Hashim. 1994. "'Tas'ir' (Price Control) in Islamic Law." *American Journal of Islamic Social Sciences* 11 (1): 25–37.

Khan, M. Fahim. 1991. "Time Value of Money and Discounting in Islamic Perspective." *Review of Islamic Economics* 1 (2): 35–45.

Khan, Muhammad Akram. 2013. *What Is Wrong with Islamic Economics? Analysing the Present State and Future Agenda*. Cheltenham, UK: Edward Elgar.

Koehler, Benedikt. 2014. *Early Islam and the Birth of Capitalism*. Idaho Falls, ID: Lexington Books.

Küçükkalay, Abdullah Mesud. 2018. *İktisadi Düşüncede Faiz* [Interest in Economic Thought]. Konya: Çizgi Kitabevi.

Kuran, Timur. 1995. "Islamic Economics and the Islamic Subeconomy." *Journal of Economic Perspectives* 9 (4): 155–73.

Miller, Robert C. B. 2015. "Price Ceilings: Ancient and Modern." In *Flaws and Ceilings: Price Controls and the Damage They Cause*, edited by Christopher Coyne and Rachel Coyne, 29–44. London: Institute of Economic Affairs.

Naqvi, Syed Nawab Haider. 2013. *Islam, Economics, and Society*. New York: Routledge.

Naqvi, Syed Nawab Haider, and Asghar Qadir. 1986. *A Model of a Dynamic Islamic Economy and the Institution of Interest*. Essays in Islamic Economic Philosophy 4. Islamabad: Pakistan Institute of Development Economics.

Olechnowicz, Cheryl A. 2011. "History of Usury: The Transition of Usury through Ancient Greece, the Rise of Christianity and Islam, and the Expansion of Long-Distance Trade and Capitalism." *Gettysburg Economic Review* 5: 97–109.

Potuzak, Pavel. 2016. "What Can We Learn from the Böhm-Bawerkian Theory in the World of Zero Interest?" *Available at SSRN 2865082*. https://ssrn.com/abstract=2865082.

Qureshi, Iqbal. 1946. *Islam and the Theory of Interest*. Lahore: Sh. M. Ashraf.

Rahman, Fazlur. 1964. "Riba and Interest." *Islamic Studies* 3 (1): 1–43.

Reifner, Udo, Sebastien Clerc-Renaud, and RA Michael Knobloch. 2010. "Study on Interest Rate Restrictions in the EU." ETD/2009/IM/H3/87. Institut für Finanzdienstleistungen.

Rougeau, Vincent D. 1996. "Rediscovering Usury: An Argument for Legal Controls on Credit Card Interest Rates." *University of Colorado Law Review* 67 (1): 1–46.

Saadallah, Ridha. 1994. "Concept of Time in Islamic Economics." *Islamic Economic Studies* 2 (1): 81–102.

Schmidtz, David. 2016. "Are Price Controls Fair?" *Supreme Court Economic Review* 23 (1): 221–33.

Schuettinger, Robert L., and Eamonn F. Butler. 1979. *Forty Centuries of Wage and Price Controls: How Not to Fight Inflation*. Washington, DC: Heritage Foundation.

Schumpeter, Joseph A. 1934. *The Theory of Economic Development*. Cambridge: Harvard University Press.

Sharawy, Hesham M. 2000. "Understanding the Islamic Prohibition of Interest: A Guide to Aid Economic Cooperation between the Islamic and Western Worlds." *Georgia Journal of International and Comparative Law* 29 (1): 153–79.

Siddique, Muhammad Abubakar, and Memoona Rahim. 2015. "The Concepts of Discounting and Time Value of Money in Islamic Capital Budgeting Framework: A Theoretical Study." *Journal of Islamic Banking and Finance* 32 (1): 23–29.

Siddiqui, Shamim Ahmad. 2006. "The Controversy over Time Value of Money among Contemporary Muslim Economists." *Journal of Management and Social Sciences* 2 (2): 144–53.

Siebert, W. Stanley. 2015. "The Simple Economics of Wage Floors." In *Flaws and Ceilings: Price Controls and the Damage They Cause*, edited by Christopher Coyne and Rachel Coyne, 45–71. London: Institute of Economic Affairs.

Thomson Reuters. 2018. "Islamic Finance Development Report."

Uludağ, Süleyman. 1988. *İslamda Faiz Meselesine Yeni Bir Bakış* [A New View on the Issue of Interest in Islam]. İstanbul: Dergah Yayınları.

Vincent, Joshua. 2014. "Historical, Religious and Scholastic Prohibition of Usury: The Common Origins of Western and Islamic Financial Practices." *Law School Student Scholarship. Paper 600.*

Visser, Wayne A. M., and Alastair McIntosh. 1998. "A Short Review of the Historical Critique of Usury." *Accounting, Business & Financial History* 8 (2): 175–189.

Zarqa, Muhammad Anas. 1982. "Capital Allocation, Efficiency and Growth in an Interest-Free Islamic Economy." *Journal of Economics and Administration, King Abdulaziz University* 16: 43–55.

———. 1983. "An Islamic Perspective on the Economics of Discounting in Project Evaluation." In *Fiscal Policy and Resource Allocation in Islam*, edited by Ziauddin Ahmed, Munawar Iqbal, and M. Fahim Khan, 179–223. Jeddah: International Centre for Research in Islamic Economics, King Abdulaziz University.

Index

C. Eyerci, *The Causes and Consequences of Interest Theory*,
https://doi.org/10.1007/978-3-030-78702-8

The manufacturer's authorised representative in the EU is Springer Nature Customer Service Centre GmbH, Europaplatz 3, 69115 Heidelberg, Germany. If you have any concerns regarding our products, please contact ProductSafety@springernature.com

Printed and bound by CPI Group (UK) Ltd, Croydon, CR0 4YY
30/09/2026
02225666-0018